Untouchable Poems

Untouchable Poems

Lived Experience with Hindu Religion, Ideology, and Society

SURYARAJU MATTIMALLA

Foreword by Oskar Schmid

RESOURCE *Publications* • Eugene, Oregon

UNTOUCHABLE POEMS
Lived Experience with Hindu Religion, Ideology, and Society

Copyright © 2024 Suryaraju Mattimalla. All rights reserved. Except for brief quotations in critical publications or reviews, no part of this book may be reproduced in any manner without prior written permission from the publisher. Write: Permissions, Wipf and Stock Publishers, 199 W. 8th Ave., Suite 3, Eugene, OR 97401.

Resource Publications
An Imprint of Wipf and Stock Publishers
199 W. 8th Ave., Suite 3
Eugene, OR 97401

www.wipfandstock.com

PAPERBACK ISBN: 979-8-3852-2803-4
HARDCOVER ISBN: 979-8-3852-2804-1
EBOOK ISBN: 979-8-3852-2805-8

VERSION NUMBER 08/07/24

To my children and wife
Stanford Suryaraju Mattimalla
Saviour Suryaraju Mattimalla
Selamawit Hailu Bezabih

To my unnamed child who was victim of Hindu's honor killing

To my parents
Patnala Suguna Yadav, alias Mattimalla Suguna Madiga
Mattimalla Titus, alias Mattimalla Anand Madiga

The lived experience of untouchable caste with Hindu, Islamic, Sikh, Buddhist, Jain, Parse, and their agents worldwide is captured in the untouchable poetry.

Contents

Foreword by Oskar Schmid | xi
Acknowledgments | xiii

Introduction | 1

1. The Origin of Untouchability | 27
2. Echoes of Exclusion | 28
3. Denied the Right to Sit before the Hindus | 30
4. Barred from the Hindu Village Well, Kept at Bay | 32
5. The Ladder Caste System | 34
6. Denied Access to the Hindu Spaces | 36
7. Untouchables Should Not Sit in Front of Hindus | 38
8. Genocide against Untouchable Castes | 40
9. Religions and Their Genocide against Untouchables | 42
10. "Untouchable" under the "Brahmin" Peshwa Rule | 44
11. King Sayajirao Gaekwad III of Baroda: A Tale of Generosity toward Ambedkar | 46
12. Philosopher Ambedkar: The Western Knowledge in Eastern Spaces | 48
13. Temple Entry Movement for Untouchables | 50
14. India's First Civil Rights Movement for Untouchable Women | 52

Contents

15. Mahad Movement for the Right to Drink Water | 54
16. Burning the Founding Father of Genocide against Untouchables: Manusmriti | 56
17. The Call For The Annihilation Of Caste | 58
18. The Ramsay Macdonald Award of 1932 for Untouchables | 60
19. Professor Dr. B. R. Ambedkar the Knowledge the Lived Experience with Humiliation | 62
20. Scavenging Caste: India's Sub-Human | 64
21. Sati: Where Wives Embraced the Funeral Pyre's Light | 66
22. The Land Where Hindu and Islamic Hearts Unite | 68
23. Traditional Marriage System: No Choice to Make, No Freedom to Rejoice | 70
24. Dowry Demands Innocent Lives | 72
25. "Madiga" Devadasis Forced into the Temple Prostitution | 74
26. Kanchikacherla Kotesu "Madiga" Massacre | 76
27. 1985 Karamchedu Carnage: The Genocide Unfolded | 78
28. 1997 Ramabai Killings: Injustice Reigned in a Ruthless Display | 80
29. Khairlanji: The Horror of September 29, 2006 | 82
30. Agony of My Mother, Suguna Yadav: Love without Borders Is to Let Love Decree | 84
31. My "Moonflower": Victim of Honor Killing | 86
32. My "Flowermoon"'Stanford: A Life Taken by Neo-Nazi Doctor | 88
33. Echoes of "Untouchable" Girl's | 90
34. Forcing Untouchable Men to Consume the World's Foul Swirl | 92
35. Influence of Western Philosophers on Ambedkar | 94
36. Threads of Humiliation | 96
37. Equality in the Writings of Western Philosophers: Rousseau, Kant, Hegel, and Smith | 98

Contents

38. Humiliation, Violence, and Degradation between Jews and Untouchables | 100
39. Janus-Faced Hindus | 102
40. Untouchable Philosophers: Ambedkar and Gopal Guru the Semi-Theoretical Lights | 104
41. American Philosopher Eleanor Zelliot: Champion of Social Justice | 106
42. American Philosopher Gail Omvedt: The Light in Darkest Space | 108
43. The Sacrifice of Madiga Dandora Voice | 110
44. Voice of "Untouchable" Women | 112
45. Voice of Queer | 113
46. The Indian Ideology | 114

Glossary | 117
Bibliography | 119

Foreword
Call for Tolerance between Religions

DURING HUMAN HISTORY so much violence and so many wars had their origin in religious intolerance!

As examples I only mention the Christian crusades of the Middle Ages and the violence caused by Islamic extremists in the modern era. To describe all the violence and all the wars initiated for religious reasons would fill books.

Particularly the monotheistic religions sometimes call people of other religions heretics or unbelievers and consider them as enemies to be persecuted or even to be killed.

Every human being has the right to believe in the God of its choice or to not believe in God!

No religion can claim its God as the only!

If all religions accepted the other religions as equal and their Gods as one among others, we would live in a not perfect, but much better world.

Oskar Schmid

Acknowledgments

I HUMBLY THANK PHILOSOPHER John Rawls for his groundbreaking work *A Theory of Justice*, which taught me the art of speaking and writing the truth. Rawls motivated me to speak and write the truth about truth and justice.

I thank Oscar Schmid for his generous help to me at various times during my asylum process in Regensburg, Germany.

I thank my German friend Johannes, who generously came and prayed in Hebrew for my son Stanford at the Christian cemetery in Dreifaltigkeitsberg, Regensburg.

I thank the Jewish community for giving me the courage to stand against caste and untouchability in a way they stand against unprecedented attacks against them for being a very decent and scientific knowledgeable community.

How can I forget my lone and dark-skinned sister, Mattimalla Vijaya Madiga, alias Mekala Vijaya Madiga, who left her education to send me to school? She worked in agricultural fields from the age of 10, along with my mother, to run my family. She married a dark-skinned Madiga husband due to the poverty of our family. Her two dark-skinned sons, Mekala Ravi and Mekala Mani, are openly discriminated against for their untouchable caste as well as for their dark skin in private and public schools in India. I am forever indebted to my sister for her sacrification, struggles, dehumanization, humiliation, casteism, and racism at the age of 13 and for helping my education. How can I say to my illiterate

Introduction

GENOCIDE MAY BE DEFINED as an internationally recognized crime where acts are committed with the intent to destroy, in whole or in part, a national, ethnic, racial, or religious group.[1] The history of the 1948 Genocide Convention could be traced to the aftermath of the Holocaust, during which the whole world saw the highest levels of atrocities and mass slaughters against the civilian population. The convention, an offspring of the Holocaust, sought to lay down an oversight framework to stop and punish acts of genocide that are the intended destruction of a national, ethnic, racial, or religious group in whole or in part. It was spearheaded by Raphael Lemkin, a Polish-Jewish lawyer and scholar. It was enacted by the UN General Assembly on December 9, 1948, and came into force on January 12, 1951. Lemkin's unceasing advocacy and scholarly output played a significant part in devising the wording of the convention because he aimed to draw the world's attention to cultural and racial elimination through the systematic murder of whole communities.

What Is Genocide?

Many scholars define genocide diversely. Schmid's study defines genocide as "any of the following acts committed with intent to destroy, in whole or in part, a national, ethnic, racial, or religious group, as such:

1. Palmer, "Genocide," 142.

a. *Killing members of the group;*

b. *Causing serious bodily or mental harm to members of the group;*

c. *Imposing measures intended to prevent births within the group;*

d. *Deliberately inflicting on the group conditions of life calculated to bring about its physical destruction in whole or in part;*

e. *Forcibly transferring the children of the group to another group.*"[2]

Schmid also defines genocide as "the denial of the right of existence of entire human groups, committed with intent to destroy, in whole or in part, a national, ethnical, racial, or religious group, as such."[3]

In Indian society, the traces of discrimination and acts of violence against a specific caste can be traced back to the ancient Vedic culture, which is probably several thousand years old. Pennington et al.'s theory on caste in politics states that the caste hierarchy (or Varna system), a foundational principle that sorted people into different rigid and hereditary job occupations for centuries, was the primary factor shaping the social order of Indian society.[4] At the peak of the hierarchy are the Brahmins, a priestly caste that takes place after Kshatriyas (warriors and rulers), Vaishyas (traders and merchants), and Shudras (laborers). Individuals who go lower than the four upper classes called Brahmins, Kshatriyas, Vaishyas, and Shudras, who are towards the bottom of the hierarchy, are called Untouchables. The social situation in India, Nepal, Sri Lanka, Pakistan, Bangladesh, Japan, Bhutan, and other parts of caste-based societies, which is characterized by the untouchability principle, which is a process of social virtualization of the Untouchable community, is the most significant focus point of caste-based oppression. In contrast, scholars may argue that, unlike the previous regime, this one ascertains certain legal

---

2. Schmid, "Repression, State Terrorism, and Genocide," 29.
3. Wakeham, "Slow Violence," 347.
4. Pennington et al., "Roundtable," 36.

the caste systems can be pinpointed by returning to the oldest scriptures, like the Manusmriti, which defined social hierarchy and set clear rules regarding inter-caste interactions. The basis of them all appeared to hail purity and pollution theories, relegate certain castes to inferior jobs, and deny them basic freedom, living rights, civil rights, human rights, social rights, educational rights, land, and social mobility.

Throughout history, the purpose of the caste system has been to create a social order based on hierarchies of power and privilege where the rule of the upper-caste and the under-caste communities is relatively marginalized and those at the bottom are disenfranchised. The imposing of caste-related occupations and restrictions against Untouchables and inter-caste marriage between Untouchables and Touchable Castes and social interactions led to the strengthening of the boundaries between these groups, as the divisions and inequality reinforced over the period. Untouchability, the prescribing of Untouchables or Madigas to the fringes of society based on the idea of their "ritual impurity," was one of the most degrading and demeaning faces of discrimination based on caste.[6] The caste system is one of the significant sources of injustice, portraying different forms of violence, inconsideration, and social degradation of Untouchables over the entire social and political history. According to Grusky's study, the legacy of the caste system inherited by the country pertains not only to "social stratification but also to the economy, politics, and culture."[7] Untouchables, whom history has labeled as the most degraded ones and deprived of all the necessities, including resources, opportunities, and human rights, suffer from a wide scale of exclusion, oppression, humiliation, degradation, rejection, reduction, isolation, excommunication, or simply in the words of political philosopher Gopal Guru, "untouchables are walking carrion, walking corpse and walking carcass."[8] Landlessness, economic backwardness, and a dearth of educational opportunities have kept successive generations of Untouchable

6. Balan, "Making of Comfortable Exile," 87.
7. Grusky, "Past, Present, and Future," 40.
8. Guru, *Humiliation*, 224.

INTRODUCTION

communities in the perpetuity of poverty and further (social) marginalization. The political representation and participation of the Untouchables are also limited by severe caste-based discrimination. This factor hinders such people from asserting their rights and interests within the democratic process.

Das's study states that the roots of oppression due to the caste system overlap with other systems of control and domination, such as "patriarchy and capitalism," which intensify the conditions of Untouchables and make people like them even more vulnerable.[9] Gender-based violence and discrimination do nothing but worsen the predicaments faced by Untouchable women, as they affect them with multifaceted discrimination based on caste, untouchability, skin color, class, and gender. Economic exploitation in the form of bonded labor and caste-based occupations is another mechanism that further consolidates the position of the Untouchables in the global capitalist economy. Caste atrocities cover the very integration of caste-based subjection and also help to understand the diversity of social injustice in India because the approach towards fighting caste-based violence should be comprehensive and intersectional. The opposition to caste-based suppression has been a critical element in India's social and political history, with Untouchable activists and leaders at the head of the movement for social justice and equality. From B. R. Ambedkar, the author of the Indian Constitution and a passionate fighter of Untouchable rights, to the recent Madiga Reservation Porata Samithi (MRPS) grassroots movement, Untouchable communities have been able to mobilize against caste-based discrimination and claim their dignity and humanity.

Echoes of Injustice

India has a varying caste system, and with such caste violence, historical scars can be seen even after several incidents that brought discrimination and oppression to the foreground of the caste

---

9. Das, "Social Oppression," 99.

system. One of these infamous events is the Kilvenmani massacre of 1968, which happened in Tamil Nadu. A group of forty-four (sixteen women, twenty-three children, and five men) Untouchable agricultural laborers were brutally murdered by landlords and upper-caste individuals for claiming wages and several working facilities.[10] The annihilation, which took the lives of males and females all through the age range of forty-four years, laid open the deep-rooted power relations and exploitation that were the hallmark of the agricultural economy, where Untouchable workers were routinely subjected to various forms of violence and exploitation. Correspondingly, the Lakshmanpur-Bathe massacre, which is ranked as one of the deadliest caste violence instances in independent India's history, was in 1997. In this savage incident, the Ranvir Sena, vacuumed in the private militia, empowered by the upper-caste landlords, came to the scene and ruthlessly inaugurated the massacre of fifty-eight Untouchables, including men, women, and children. The massacre, which specifically aimed at Untouchable farm workers and their families, was brought about by the hate involving caste identity and the desire to hold the Hindu positions in the region as per the social and economic hegemony. Despite the horrendous nature of the crime, the guilty have not been amenable to law and justice and have directly ridiculed the victims and survivors, reflecting the heinous impunity that potentiates caste-based violence.

In 1979–1980, Bhagalpur blindings—another disgusting manifestation of caste violence—involved the blinding of over thirty Untouchables by police officers in the town of Bhagalpur, Bihar, with the use of acid or sand. The sad part of it was that the victims, who were primarily poor agricultural laborers, were utterly humiliated, brutalized, and mutilated for their participation in a protest against the local authorities.[11] The event, which inflamed people's anger and even disgust, showed that the state authorities knew about the situation but did not want to stop the practices of

---

10. Gough, "Indian Peasant Uprisings," 1391–1412; Rahman, "Question of Identity," 30.

11. Mukherjee and Chakraborty, "Disturbing Trend," 125.

caste-based discrimination and violence, as well as the way power could be used against the weaker communities.

The recurrent instances of casteism in India are not isolated incidents, but they are the filament of everyday life across the country for Untouchable castes. The acts of discrimination in manual scavenging, where the Untouchables must clean human waste with their own hands, are still occurring even after these are not legally allowed. The news of caste-based atrocities like rape, murder, and social boycotts still seems to persist in alerts, confirming the chronic influence that caste-based discrimination and violence leave on Indian society as a whole.

According to Chakraborty's theory of work engagement, the interplay of caste-based violence with other forms of marginalization, including gender-based violence and economic exploitation, also makes the job of the Untouchable communities challenging and complex.[12] In terms of Untouchable women, they experience disparate caste-based violence that is, in turn, characterized by intersecting forms of discrimination based on caste, skin color, class, and gender. With Untouchable feminisms, a response to the issues that are peculiar to Untouchable women and which stress the intersectional nature of the problems that they face has been raised, with an added component of holistic approaches to dealing with the cases of casteism and sexism, among other such types of vices.

Colonial Legacies

The colonial era in India, which lasted for nearly two hundred years of British colonial administration, had a profound impact on the country's social, political, and economic fabric, and the caste system was one of the most affected. However, British colonial rule did not behave as a neutral umpire to the caste system. On the contrary, it consciously used caste for administrative convenience and economic interest. The emergence of census surveys and the legal conceptualization of castes, together with the codification

---

12. Chakraborty, "Gendered Violence," 667.

of customary laws and practices, were the factors that enshrined caste-based identities and hierarchies, giving way to caste discrimination and marginalization.

The repercussion of colonialism on caste dynamics, which landed as the establishment of the "divide and rule" policy by British colonial authorities, is that they intentionally benefited from and promoted different castes' internal hostility to command and control and put down protests. It achieved this by employing selective favoritism and privileges for specific traditional Hindu groups, particularly Brahmins and other powerful clans of the day.[13] As such, this was done, in part, to incorporate local elites and, second, to create power bases for the colonial administration. In this way, the system of castes was not only preserved, but new divisions were intensifying between the castes, enabling the system of violence and oppression to reign over Indian society cyclically.

The land governance and agrarian reforms introduced by the British colonial state prolonged caste divisions, primarily through land tenure systems that privileged certain higher-caste landowners against Untouchable farm laborers. The imposition of revenue systems and the policies of taxation excessively load poorer areas, specifically marginalized communities, exacerbating their condition by leaving them without resources and making them incapable of escaping from the ownership of Hindu, Muslim, Sikh, Jain, Parse, and Buddhist landlords. The concentration of land possession under British colonial regulation, alongside the planting of cash crops by the British, as well as the advent of commercial agriculture, intensified the situation, which ended up with the marginalization and economic exploitation of the Untouchable community.

Local government's adoption of differentiating attitudes and actions towards Untouchables by colonial officials perpetuated prejudice, dislikes, and stereotypes, which favored sidelining and stigmatization. Untouchables were subjugated to the merciless caste system; exposed to violence; denied education, jobs, and political representation; and pushed to the bottom of society. The colonial state of the British was not the one that was cleansed of

---

13. Lee, "Historical Inequality," 183.

untouchability by their policies and practices but instead was the one that directly and indirectly strengthened caste-based discrimination and oppression, which led to the marginalization of Untouchable communities.

Social inequalities, discrimination, and violence do not disappear even after the departure of the colonial masters; Hinduism, Brahmanism, and colonialism remains to influence the caste dynamics in contemporary India. The end of British rule and the independence following did not come about with the issue of inequalities and power imbalances. What was inherited from colonialism reincarnates and affects caste-based discrimination and oppression through different avenues. An ostensible post-colonial Indian state, "despite being presumably dedicated to social justice and equality,"[14] is unable to resolve the key elements that cause caste-based violence and discrimination that result in reinforcing the cycles of marginalization and injustice.

Untouchability-Based Violence as Genocide

Breaking the Silence

Indian untouchability-based violence has been around for a long time, an embedded form of prejudice in the caste system, free from history. According to Kumar's study, the term "untouchability" identifies a social institution responsible for legitimizing and incorporating discriminatory ideologies against some social groups and oppressing them through their enforcement mechanisms.[15] For the caste system, the Untouchable community in South Asia, as it is known today, experienced the atrocities that a feudalization system could gain. However, the practice or intergenerational undergoing of "untouchability" or "caste discrimination" takes place unofficially even after the legal ratification of the abolition of

---

14. The Constitution of Indian articles 14 and 15.

15. Kumar, "Impact of Dr. Ambedkar's Philosophy on International Activism of the Dalit Diaspora," 1.

untouchability. However, the gravity of violence directed against Untouchables for thousands of years has not substantially been explored, and its overview of ethnic cleansing has not been recognized. It is high time now to stop the hush around atrocities based on untouchability and accurately define those offenses internationally.

Untouchability created a rigid caste system. This caste system put the Untouchable castes even below the lowest Varna. It was thought that the polluting effects of their touch or shadow made them impure. Scholars like Karl Marx, Ambedkar, Eleanor Zelliot, Gail Omvedt, Gnana Aloysious, Gopal Guru, Anand Teltumbde, Perry Anderson, Chinnaiah Jangam, Sharmila Rege, Sambaiah Gundimeda, and Rao argue that, denoted as "unclean" or "untouchable," Untouchables were subjected to social isolation and limited access to education and occupations, as well as their limited ability to own property and the freedom to pray or mingle with other castes. However, social fabric regulations that limit a group's ability to thrive and continue their existence over generations also arise due to such conditions. The routine atrocities included horrifying public lashings, parading naked, compelling the defiant to eat the filthiest substances, such as human excrement, and merciless lynching over trivial disputes or mere suspicion of polluting Hindu castes. They imposed that children were not left out of such misery either.

Although the most widely spread and horrific form of discrimination has been honor killings and gang rapes against Untouchable women and men, they are used incessantly for the living ammunition of a community. Even unfounded rumors of any Untouchable girl who might brush the path of a Hindu caste person may bring out an agitated community to strip, gang rape in public, and then lynch the girl with impunity. The Untouchable women's reputation of being just sexual objects remorselessly used by the Hindu males reinforces this process by disempowering thousands. These kinds of processes of dehumanization follow a pattern seen too many times before. Apart from the discrimination and the lack of access to law enforcement and justice institutions that are supposed to protect marginalized groups from different ideologies that have degradation as their main aim, it crosses the line between mere discrimination and the violation of human dignity.

Researchers like Pandey and Mishra argue that some acts of violence are designed not only to put down or keep Untouchables economically down but also to exterminate them through selective killing.[16] Affronts to humanity, such as entire Untouchable ghettos being set on fire where police officers collude or stand idly by, qualify as crimes against humanity (Karamchedu massacre, Kanchikacherla Kotesu massacre, etc.). Hence, this is also analogous to besieging behavior when a noncomplying group is denied not only medical aid but also other vital resources and safety measures, and this often leads to the natural deaths of vulnerable groups like children, the elderly, and those who are ill or pregnant without polluting the male members of a higher caste society.

A terrible thing is even more fascinating given the growing reports that many human bodies have been found in various parts of India in a large number of graves that were hidden for years. The DNA match corroborated that most of the murders were Untouchables. Such mass extermination and disposal of the bodies with impunity or extended toleration reveals the long-existing and accepted culture of atrocities against the oppressed. The names, the dates, the places, and the calls for justice are now known and are dealt with as untouchability-based crimes against humanity and even potential cases of genocide under the 1948 Convention.

Unveiling the Horror

Khairlanji Massacre (2006)

The Khairlanji massacre in Maharashtra, India, is a bone-chilling incident that saw the killings of some lower caste family members eventually turn ghastly into genocide. In 2006, a dreadful incident happened where a family of Untouchables consisting of four members was brutally murdered by a group of an upper caste that was

16. Pandey and Mishra, "Dalit Women's Narratives," 319.

supposed to be based on a land dispute. The incident gave birth to widespread protests and anger, which represent the natural prevailing hierarchies and casteist attitudes that persist in Indian society to date. Initially, the state hesitated to identify this case as genocide, and the proceedings were slow, which proves the difficulty of naming and handling caste-motivated violence.

Laxmanpur Bathe Massacre (1997)

The Lakshmanpur Bathe massacre in Bihar, India, was one more awful case of a massacre by caste-based atrocity. In 1997, an uppercase activist band violently disrupted a Untouchable hamlet. Sixty-eight Untouchable human lives, including fifteen women and fourteen children, lost their lives. The Untouchables' rising urge to assert themselves and their desire for land share were the reasons for the massacre that was directed as retaliation.

Bhim Army Attacks (2017)

The Bhim Army, a Untouchable rights group in the state of Uttar Pradesh in India, endured some violent attacks in 2017, and it is suspected that the Hindu castes instigated these attacks. These attacks were directed against the Untouchable communities and their leaders in particular, which was aimed at preventing the latter's fight for social justice. The event indicates that caste-based violence is here to stay, and immediate steps are required to be taken to treat the cause of such violence.

Caste-Based Discrimination in Nepal

The Untouchables of Nepal, together with the marginalized groups, persistently suffer social and physical discrimination, which is based on the hierarchies that are guarded by caste. Although the constitution of Nepal abolished the caste system, it has rarely perished, thus spurring cases of violence, marginalization, and discrimination. While the Nepalese government's effort in tackling caste-based discrimination and violence appears first, this issue leads to more severe problems that are recognized and treated on a South Asian scale.

Genocide Unveiled

The 1948 Convention

The 1948 Genocide Convention is an international treaty that defines that genocide is a crime punished by criminal prosecution and that it is necessary for member countries to enforce its prohibition. It was the first law case that defined genocide as a crime and the first human rights treaty endorsed on December 9, 1948, unanimously by the United Nations with all General Assembly members. The convention began on January 12, 1951, and reached 2022, with the belligerent countries 152. As outlined in the convention, genocide is "any of the following five offenses committed with the specific purpose of bringing about the total or partial annihilation of a national, ethnical, racial, or religious group."[17] After the horrible consequences of World War II, where millions of civilians were killed in an organized attempt to eliminate certain groups, the international community approached the issue of controlling the mistreatment of minority groups by institutionalizing a set of rules.

NGOs or other organizations representing victims of these genocides interviewed world leaders to condemn and prohibit such atrocities. With aerial photos of wartime extermination camps, mass graves, and the systematically organized elimination of Jews, Roma, Slavs, homosexuals, persons with disabilities, and those critical of the Nazi government, the Holocaust and other genocidal acts were pointed out to the whole world.[18] Everything that witnesses had to say was almost unbearable, and the witnesses narrated the brutal killings and massacres that they had not only

17. Article 2 of the UNO Genocide Convention.
18. Brown, *Forgotten German Genocide*, 79.

witnessed but also experienced. Pictures and films, in this case, had the sole purpose of highlighting crude facts to the world. There was an increasing realization that such atrocities should not happen again. Thus, it came about that the name of this new order in the judgment of nations was "United Nations."

In 1948, officials from fifty nations met in Paris at the Palais de Chaillot to develop a contemporary international treaty. Participants scrutinized documentation, pictures, and written testimonies by groups like the World Jewish Congress so that they could better comprehend the significance of the horrific events. It turned out to be more than such mass murdering the history of the human race could recall. For instance, the Nazis murdered more than six million Jews in different countries, with the majority of their victims being European Jews. The same fate befell the Roma community, as the population of over 220,000 who perished was reported based on research. Groups pressed the most challenging legal instrument that not only branded such crimes but encompassed undertakings of all states to avert and punish subsequent genocides. During long and exhausting negotiations, the Convention on the Prevention and Punishment of Genocide Crime was approved on behalf of each participant.

The 1948 Genocide Convention was the one that was to put in writing and spearhead the definition of genocide and specify several prohibited activities. The resolution resolved that "at the best possible times in history, genocide has inflated losses to humanity."[19] Later, it is defined as the reaching of the goal of killing members, undertaking measures to prevent births, or forcibly transferring children to this national, ethnic, racial, or religious group by the use of these actions. Parties would be compelled by the terms of the treaty to call for and enforce the punishment of the crime of genocide, whether or not it was committed in war or peace. However, controversially, the rule did not embrace political groups as sheltering, the main factor that bothered the defenders. It became a turning point for the world community when the international community unanimously proclaimed universal human

---

19. Wilson, *Writing History in International Criminal Trials*, 115–16.

INTRODUCTION

rights and exclaimed, to the worst of all, that this crime should never be repeated.

In its aftermath, the statistics of the case seem to prove that genocide and all its horrors are a fact. The Khmer Rouge regime achieved power in Cambodia in 1975. Also, it enacted policies that caused 1.5 to 3 million deaths out of eight million of the total population through starvation, medical neglect, execution, or labor exhaustion—that meant 25 percent of the country's total population. In Rwanda, during 1994, usually the ethnic Tutsi and moderate Hutu political groups constituting five hundred thousand to one million people were killed by the Hutu fanatics in one hundred days. Both cases pointed out the shortfall of the international community to halt during the evolution of atrocities, while the "genocide" obligation was set in 1948. However, despite these prevention criteria's original purpose and effectiveness, intervention mechanisms and accountability were still debatable.

Implementing the convention early on and enforcing the agreement posed significant challenges. Around eighty states initially voted for the protocol, but putting the agreements into practice and turning them into actions was way more complicated. Strong powers tended to be uncooperative when harming their irreducible interests and were often unwilling to take action, even against widely known perpetrators of genocide or other crimes against humanity. Finally, legal proceedings were beset with multiple obstacles since specifically proving that there was genocidal intent in the court of law was a procedure of almost impossible difficulty. Nevertheless, we had the creation of the UN Office of the Special Adviser on the Prevention of Genocide and the founding of the International Criminal Tribunal for Rwanda (ICTR), which was initiated after the 1994 genocide to prosecute the perpetrators. The twenty-first century saw not only geographically expansive but also technologically enhanced tools for the timely precaution of sensitive zones due to new technology and further committee procedures.

The Genocide Convention, adopted over seventy-five years ago, is still the critical document setting forth the individual criminal liability and responsibility of the state concerning the crime of genocide. Nevertheless, gaps and deficiencies are there. Some countries still have not ratified it. No mechanism is implemented to ensure prevention or intervention when risks increase. The political will to enforce the convention on principles through sanctions or military action is feeble. Establishing universal jurisdiction for prosecution has its deficiencies. The continuing cases, such as the October 7 modern holocaust in Israel and ethnic violence in places such as South Sudan and the Tigray Region in Ethiopia, show both the convention's enduring relevance and its limitations without follow-through.

In overviewing how these historical events unfolded—from the horrors that triggered the adoption of the Genocide Convention to its current effects and shortcomings nearly seventy-five years later—a few lessons emerge. It first shows that simply having a legal framework in place is meaningless if there is no political will and timely action on the attack on genocide that is usually wanted. It demonstrated that governments may become more reactive and open to policy adjustments when awakenings and constant pressure from advocates take place. Ultimately, the International Criminal Tribunal on Rwanda for the punishment of genocide serves as a pointer that, completely with new laws, norms, and tribunals, genocide shall remain a threat as long as there are societies that condone messaging that dehumanizes "the other" and leaders believe they can enact policies of social re-engineering with impunity. Humanity alone can craft a world in which there is no genocide with the recognition of the rights of all humans. However, the convention is a significant milestone in the journey towards preventing similar genocides in the future, which is still incomplete.

INTRODUCTION

Unmasking Global Injustice: International Failures and Lobbying Dynamics

The Blind Eye: UNO and International Human Rights Bodies

The failure of the United Nations (UN) and any other international body of human rights to recognize caste genocide in India exposes a persistent oversight in dealing with pervasive discrimination and violence against which marginalized communities wage a tough battle. Though documents showing the ignominious crimes done towards Untouchables and other oppressed social groups may exist, the world community seems to be unaware of the intensity of caste violence and its genocidal implications. The very fact that official reports do not acknowledge caste genocide at large further paves the way for immunity and unfairness in society, thus giving the perpetrators a place to hide from their crimes in the range of impunity.[20] National organizations ignore the question of caste genocide by international bodies not only to condone the rights and dignity of affected communities but also to contribute to a culture of silence and collaboration in the wake of state-backed discrimination.

Genocide-defining documents of caste atrocities have been facing deaf ears from UNO and other allied associations for a long time. This act of noninvestigation proves the suffering of many Untouchable victims and evokes further abuse. Be it in 1950 or later, Dr. Ambedkar, one of the famous Untouchable leaders, felt the need to petition the UNO, enumerating impunity against Untouchables as a form of socioreligious genocide that should cause serious intervention. Nonetheless, it turned deaf ears and was unacknowledged without any action. During the several years after, one can find more evidence from Untouchable rights organizations that meticulously documented the long-standing human treatment and campaigns of extermination at the UNO. Even though caste is undoubtedly not included in the UNO approaches that are applied for the redress of injustice and human rights.

20. Khan, "It Is Not Possible," 280.

Other UN mechanisms like the CERD and individual rapporteurs have not explicitly used the forces in their duty or country visions to investigate apparent signs of caste-based discrimination turning into genocidal in India, Nepal, Sri Lanka, Pakistan, Bangladesh, Japan, Tibet, and other parts of caste-world. At worst, they sound like benign acknowledgments without even a hint of the systemic socio-cultural-religious-political connotations of caste and the targeted lethal nature of social discrimination. Even more painful is the fact that the highest officials deny caste racial discrimination against all the legal evidence of the issue. As such, this contravenes the principles of UN universal equality and nondiscrimination. It implies more to the victims that their lives are of little value and does not even elicit a mere apology after murderous attacks.

Even after many prompting events to broaden knowledge, the absence of UNO driving caste crime prevention activities stresses whether international law will be upheld without political prejudice. One of the many instances was when it refused to dispatch fact-finding teams after the large-scale pogroms in Jhajjar lynching, Khairlanji carnage, Karamchedu masscre, Chundur carnage, or Dharmapuri carnage, where hundreds of Untouchables were raped and killed. Compare this with the wit and volition shown in other similar areas, like the genocide in Rwanda or comparatively recent occupation contexts. We might ask, "Why can't the seismic effect of human destruction in caste violence incidents generate the need to involve international global citizens?" For instance, such impunity and the selective application of human rights standards caste doubt on the universality of human rights principles.

The compliance of interworld organizations to caste massacres through the use of many political reasons and power is also one of the factors that laid the foundation of this kind of genocide. The role of the Indian lobby in global committees, including at the UN, affected global standards for caste discrimination, and there have not been convincing measures taken to contain caste-based violence. Caste violence is frequently overshadowed by the high-profile achievements of the government and its supporters in their power lobbying. It is because these barbarically cruel people remain

Introduction

undisturbed. Such a biased generation of global narratives and policies further translates into Untouchables continuing to be marginalized and destabilizing the credibility and power of international human rights mechanisms to mitigate systemic discrimination.

Lobbying Power Play: The Indian Lobby's Global Reach

The caste-based disparity globally has emerged as a geopolitical tool of influence among the world powers. The well-established interest group is a major player in setting the agenda for resolving this complex issue at the UN, in the USA, and in the EU. Via this tactical approach, the lobby is responsible for framing the narrative and policy outcomes molded for its own good. This process somehow blurs out the pleas for recognition of casteism as a form of genocide formulated by Untouchable activists at the international level. The community can utilize its financial and diplomatic standings to cast the local voices of Untouchables away from the international stage and the forum. Consequently, the following global discourse and actions aimed at caste-based atrocity prevention have not been sufficient to stamp out this systemic social oppression, as contended by some Untouchable rights activists. The Indian lobby utilizes sophisticated tactics from within global institutions to influence the general direction of the world's affairs.[21] For instance, the USA had recruited lobbying businesses to present their point of view in favor of India to the Democratic lawmakers who criticized the Kashmir decision and the CAA (Citizenship Amendment Act). Through diplomacy and economic interactions, the nexus has successfully influenced the course of events in the international arenas, which today happen to be leaning towards the interests of the Indian state rather than the vast majority of the Indians, who happen to be Untouchables. To illustrate, Indian officials have used their area of influence in an attempt to erase evidence linking caste-based violence to genocide. Work was also done to prevent this matter related to human rights violations from being a periodic subject on the agendas of

21. Manulak, "Sources of Influence," 26.

leading United Nations and other such bodies. Governments, as well as international organizations twining up to carry out such practices, get little accountability for discrimination and misconduct towards Untouchables across the globe.

The Indian lobby has not only been successful in global discourse by not only allowing critical reasons for caste-based discrimination but also through how it has managed to censor all negative evaluations of the discrimination. For example, the Indian state neglected the UN's attempt to recognize caste-based discrimination among issues of racial discrimination, even though it is precancerous to racial discrimination based on possible notions of purity and pollution. What is more, the Indian lobby has also experienced outstanding accomplishments in their efforts to overlook the recognition of caste violence as a form of genocide, although this acknowledgment would provide a legal approach to dealing with the issue internationally. Indian lobby groups further substantiate their international influence through their role in promulgating the international community's efforts to combat caste-based discrimination. For instance, the Indian lobby made the UN abandon the resolution on caste-based discrimination, although such a resolution would provide the framework for dealing with the cases at the international level. Another sign of the Indian lobby's impact on global discourse manifests in India's capability to silence debate about the Indian government's reaction to caste-based discrimination. For instance, the Indian government has successfully prevented the UN from criticizing its handling of caste-based discrimination, although the government's response to the problem is insufficient in addressing the issue.

India's Maneuvering in International Forums

India's diplomatic maneuvering in international forums regarding caste-based discrimination incorporates a fine art of forming strategic alliances as well as exerting diplomatic and narrative framing demands to safeguard its interests and suppress further scrutiny of its human rights record.

Introduction

Diplomatic Pressure

India utilizes its diplomacy to neutralize other people's voices, so India will not be held responsible for the caste system. When negotiating bilaterally and multilaterally, India makes sure that it is independent and that no foreigner interferes with national affairs; this includes the issue of caste-based discrimination, which is proclaimed to be domestic and not supranational. Along with the country, the world actors do not give an explicit message not to criticize case discrimination, but via indirect messages are sent, and thus, the stage for the problems that require the United Nations intervention is set up.

Strategic Alliances

India promotes partnerships with countries with similar values and like-minded regional blocs to strengthen its diplomatic role and face attempts to tackle caste schemes head-on at international platforms. Through making partnerships with countries that have the same attitude towards sovereignty and noninterference, India may multiply its weight and thwart the initiatives aimed at spotlighting caste atrocities on the global agenda. Through these alliances, India can exert collective (and sometimes successful) pressure and construct narratives that privilege national sovereignty over human rights concerns, undermining initiatives aiming at holding it to account concerning its position on caste-based discrimination.

Economic Leverage

India's economic power, which includes its market potential, grants it undeniable influence in the international sphere, leading to foreign powers and organizations not even thinking about posting criticisms of caste injustices. India's economic enlightenment may be able to increase compliance and raise the voices against caste-based discrimination globally by penalizing people who do not adhere to its policies. Many big corporations want to make a fortune from the Indian people and their investments, so during this process, they will not talk harmlessly about India's human rights problems; they are afraid of what might happen to their business.

Media Manipulation

India uses its media control and bias in its foreign policy in order to influence opinion in the international arena regarding caste discrimination and repressive dissenting opinions. Through state-controlled media channels and the strategic communication approaches of the Indian government, instances of caste atrocities tend to be portrayed as politically driven and sensationalized, dislodging the systemic problems and human rights issues at hand. In an attempt to deny the effects of caste discrimination, India tries to face all criticism and, at the same time, presents itself as a world player committed to human rights and social justice.[22]

Diplomatic Deflections

India employs diplomatic deflections to shift the focus from caste atrocities to other matters, such as more acceptable or politically expedient ones. With a framework on caste discrimination within the broader subjects of poverty eradication, social development, and cultural diversity, India gives a twist to criticism and sugarcoats the seriousness of caste-based violence and discrimination. Crafty diplomacy, which is coupled with a sound messaging system, enables the country to distort the truth about caste atrocities and evade responsibility on the world stage.

The State's Oppression of Untouchable Voices

The Untouchables' resistance, which asks for equality and social justice, is answered by the Indian state, which suppresses it through diverse means and drives to preserve the caste system's hierarchy.

22. Thakur, "New Media."

INTRODUCTION

State-Sponsored Repression

The government of India implemented specific legislation and administrative and extra-formal (nonconstructive) ways to control and suppress Untouchable activism and dissent. The arbitrary detentions are mostly done under harsh laws. The most popular one is the Unlawful Activities (Prevention) Act (UAPA), which is the channel they use to shush Untouchable leaders and activists who speak their minds and believe that their way of thinking can pose a threat to the institutions. Endowments of authoritative bodies of law enforcement establish means like surveillance and intimidation to create fear in Untouchables and to restrict them, including associations, from questioning the old system of hierarchy of caste-based discrimination by which they are discriminated.

Media Manipulation

The state media, having a dominant position, attempts to produce stereotypes and label Untouchable activists and organizations as anti-national or subversive elements. It puts a veil on biases and selectively frames the state, which makes Untouchable movements for social equality threats to national unity and security, thus making repressive measures against Untouchable activists legitimate. Through the control of the narrative where Untouchables voice dissent, the state needles down public perception and provides it with an excuse for maintaining order in the name of social unrest, which it fabricates itself.

Structural Discrimination

Caste-based discriminatory laws, regulations, and norms lead to the establishment of the Untouchables' marginalization and the detriment of their quest for justice within the Indian legal and sociopolitical system. Notwithstanding the enshrined constitutional guarantees of equality and nondiscrimination, Untouchables are affected by the system of institutionalized informal mechanisms that continue to disremember their rights and prevent accessibility to justice. Environmental inequality is expressed in different situations, such as employment, healthcare, and education selectivity, as well as in perpetuations of the caste biases of the state systems. It not only reinforces the Untouchable dependency, which brings them more into the brackets of state-supported repression and violence, but also desolates their individuality and agency.

Global Solidarity

International solidarity plays a significant role because it strengthens the movement of people to aid Untouchable rights and ensure that Untouchable communities in India are not victims of structural discrimination. The role of international human rights organizations, civil society groups, and advocacy networks has been crucial in publicizing Untouchable rights issues and challenging the authority of the Indian lobby. An example of a successful campaign is #UntouchableLivesMatter. This banner brought global attention and comprehensive support for Untouchable rights.[23] These accomplishments have not only brought to light the fate of Untouchable communities but also demanded actions from governments and inter-state organizations against discrimination in terms of one's caste. Working on strategies for strengthening international unity and cooperation is necessary to diminish the power of Indian lobbyists and advance the struggle for Untouchable rights on the world stage. As such, this includes fostering cooperation or partnerships between Untouchable rights organizations, human rights advocates, and grassroots movements to make those advocacy efforts more effective by sharing resources and amplifying collective voices. As well as tackling policymakers, diplomats, and institutions, we need to bring the issue of the violation of Untouchable rights to the international human rights agenda as a fundamental step towards the complete mainstreaming of caste-based discrimination as a global human rights issue. Coalition building across boundaries

---

23. Thakur, "New Media," 366.

and solidarity among countries create a support structure through which the international community as a whole can make a contribution that is meaningful and just.

Towards Recognition and Action

In bringing back the shadows of caste-based discrimination and untouchability in the examination, there are some key facts and insights after this study. The first fact that emerges is that caste discrimination in India has profound roots and is still a nourishing discriminatory system against the Untouchable population. Leveraging the perspective of history, we illuminate the origins of oppression inherent in colonial inheritances and age-old caste structures that have decisively molded the sociopolitical shape of contemporary India. On top of this, our investigation shows how the state in India, assisted by influential lobbies, helps to stifle Untouchable voices and allows a culture of impunity in connection with caste violence to perpetuate. From sponsoring state repression to media manipulation as well as structural discrimination, which are complex and deeply rooted, they are thus very challenging to the realization of Untouchable rights and justice.

Through this analysis, it becomes clear that action and recognition of this discrimination are paramount to all human rights. For many generations, different groups fought against caste discrimination, but incidents of caste attacks happened even more often, with no one being punished and some of the victims left out of the community. The most important thing is for the international community to listen to the Untouchable rights activists's voices and give them an avenue to be heard in front of the world. Hence, by showing the moony area of caste discrimination and untouchability, we can engineer public opinion to bring about changes in the existing system. Only by seriously working to break away from caste discrimination and giving importance to all as equal to each other will the land of the free become a reality. By highlighting the horrendous marginalization of Untouchables in India, the international community gets a terrible wake-up call, urging it to seek involvement and assistance. Therefore, it would be pivotal for the international community to recognize caste-based discrimination as an essential human rights matter that now demands urgent attention and action. The Untouchables are characteristically maltreated and subjected to violence, necessitating stringent measures from national governments, nongovernmental organizations, and the international community. The refusal to acknowledge and tackle caste injustice not only creates pain for millions of people but also goes against the equality and justice principles founded as the core of international human rights doctrines.

Thus the "Untouchable" poetry from the lived experience will elevate the voices of the untouchable community who have historically faced genocidal persecution, discrimination, and oppression in this context of genocidal persecution against four hundred million Untouchables across the Asian-Pacific-MENA-African spaces. Poems about the Untouchables are a potent way to convey their experiences, hardships, goals, and defiance. The spirit of untouchable poetry is a powerful reflection of resistance and perseverance. Buffeting strengthens and fortifies, refining via hardships known as paeans and heaping onto a community. These are poems written by poets urging people to band together in the fight against repressive systems that harm individuals and promote social justice. Although the status of Untouchables is reflected in most untouchable poetry, there is also a hope and goal for a just society that defies it. Poets imagined a day when individuals would be treated with self-respect and be released from these cruel caste-based practices.

1. The Origin of Untouchability

In shadows of ancient realms, where Caste's cruel might unfurl,
Hindu religion birthed Untouchables,[24] a plight that time hurls.[25]
Stratified society, a rigid caste divide,
Untouchables emerged in shadows, and they'd abide.
Medieval times, under the crescent moon's gaze,
Muslim rule, a different era, yet Untouchables in a daze.
Discrimination persisted, though rulers changed attire,
Untouchability endured, a persistent, haunting fire.
In modern times, the British grasp a colonial hold,
Yet, Untouchables remained in stories untold.[26]
Subjugation morphed a foreign master's reign,
But the Untouchables' status is an unbroken chain.
Contemporary winds blew, post-1947's light,
Hindu rule regained, yet Untouchables in plight.
Unseeable, untouched, unshadowable, unapproachable still,
The echoes of ancient wounds, the present can't distill.
Through epochs, their shadows, unyielding and stark,
Untouchables endured in history's dark arc.
Unseen, unheard, unshadow they tread,
A timeless struggle in society's thread.[27]

---

24. According to Gopal Guru, "untouchables are walking carrion, walking carcass, and walking corpse"; Guru, *Humiliation*, 224.

25. Ambedkar, *Babasaheb Ambedkar Writings and Speeches* (hereafter BAWS), 7:249.

26. BAWS, 7:250.

27. BAWS, 7:251.

2. Echoes of Exclusion

In the shadows, they roam unseen, unheard,
Walking carrion,[28] their voices deferred.
Their steps heavy with the weight of disdain,
In a world where acceptance is but a feigned refrain.[29]
Walking carcass,[30] they traverse the land,
Marked by society's unforgiving hand.
Their dreams lie shattered, their hopes entwined,
In a system that leaves them far behind.

Walking corpse,[31] a label they bear,
But within them, resilience lingers, rare.
Their spirits flicker amidst the gloom,
A beacon of light in the gathering doom.
Living dead in a world so cold,
Their stories remain untold, untold.
They carry the burden of centuries past,
Injustice etched in each step, steadfast.[32]
Yet still they rise, their voices strong,
In the face of oppression, they march along.
Walking carrion, yet alive in their plea,
For a world where all are truly free.

---

28. Guru, *Humiliation*, 19, 224.
29. Keer, *Life and Mission*, 4.
30. Guru, *Humiliation*, 19, 224.
31. Guru, *Humiliation*, 19, 224.
32. Keer, *Life and Mission*, 5.

Walking carcass, in a society unkind,
But within them, a spirit refined.
They challenge the norms; they break the mold,
Their courage is a tale waiting to be told.
Despite being a walking corpse,
they demonstrate the need for perseverance.
In a culture that embraces variety with demeaning it,
Every "touchable" is respected. Every "sacred" is appreciated and valued in this society.

Despite appearing to be the Walking Corpse, Unseeable[33] remains positive.[34]
We are confident that future generations will be greater,
with everyone achieving their goals and no one falling short.
While listening to their muted pleas, we must be compassionate.
Their struggles help us understand our own, and by working together,
we can build a new universe.

---

33. In caste society, the unseeable is defined as untouchable, unshadowable, unapproachable, and unspeakable. Seeing an untouchable person's face in the early hours of the day bears a death sentence from the Sacred Castes and its operatives. Sacred caste foot soldiers wield greater authority than Brahmin "Manudharma Shasra" when it comes to administering social penalties to those who are untouchable. Analysis is mine.

34. Keer, *Life and Mission*, 6

3. Denied the Right to Sit before the Hindus

In the shadows of injustice, they silently tread.
Untouchables, burdened by the weight of dread,
Denied the right to sit before the higher Caste,[35]
Their presence was deemed unworthy, a memory to erase.
Footwear is forbidden; their soles are left bare.
In a world where privilege taints the air,
Forced to walk on paths of dust and stone,
Their dignity was trampled, and their worth was unknown.
Hindu localities, forbidden terrain,
Untouchables barred, their freedom waned,
Invisible barriers, walls of disdain,
Their existence was shunned, their rights in vain.
Water, a source of life and a symbol of hope,
But for the Untouchables, a cruelly tightened rope
Banned from the wells, from rivers flowing free,
Their thirst was unquenched in a caste-stricken plea.
Love, a forbidden fruit beyond their grasp,
Forbidden to cherish, forbidden to clasp,
Their hearts are confined in love's forbidden dance,
Prejudice's lance shackled their desires.
The speech was silenced, voices choked with fear.
In the presence of higher castes, they disappear.
Their words unspoken, their thoughts confined,
In a world where inequality is enshrined.[36]

35. Thorat, "Oppression and Denial," 572.
36. In Asia-Pacific, Africa, and the Middle East and North Africa, Untouchables are still not permitted to sit in front of Hindus, Muslims, Buddhists,

White cloths, a symbol of purity's light,
But for the Untouchables—a veil of blight,
Denied the right to wear, in front of those deemed high,
Their identity was stifled beneath a casteist sky.
Ninety-eight shackles, binding tight,
Untouchables trapped in discrimination's blight,
Yet amidst the darkness, a flicker of hope
A call for justice, a struggle to cope.
For Untouchables to rise, resilient and bold,
Their voices echo, breaking the mold.
Demanding rights long denied, ignored,
In their battle for equality, their spirits soared.

Sikhs, Jains, or Parses. In fact, untouchability is still strictly enforced against Untouchable Castes everywhere caste is practiced. This is a transnational breach of the Genocide Convention of 1948. For thousands of years, Untouchable Castes have been the target of genocidal persecution due to caste and untouchability. Analysis is mine.

4. Barred from the Hindu Village Well, Kept at Bay

In shadows cast by ancient norms, they dwell.
Bound by taboos, the stories they tell,
Untouchables, relegated to the fray,
Barred from the village well, kept at bay.[37]
Their vessels shunned, forbidden to draw,
From waters deemed pure, an unequal law.
Outside the bounds of city, town, and square,
In ghettos marked by Caste, they bear their share.
Not bound by faith, nor creed, nor creed's accord,
But by the labels cast by Caste's sharp sword.
Hindu, Muslim, Jain, Sikh, or Parsee,
Their place is set where others cannot see it.
Their homes lie distant, separate, and apart.
From the centers of power, a world apart.
Untouchable ghettos, their stark abode,
Where echoes of discrimination corrode.[38]
Even beyond India's sacred ground,[39]

37. BAWS, vol. 3.
38. BAWS, vol. 3.
39. My understanding from empirical study is that, in their various theoretical and empirical research societies and places, even castes affiliated with the United Nations, Amnesty International, Human Rights Watch, or knowledge centers in Cambridge, Oxford, and Colombia, engage in untouchability and raw-based casteism against Untouchable Castes. Even in western settings, the practice of untouchability has become commonplace. "Castes of mind" are defined as omnipresence and omnipotence throughout "theoretical and emperical space and time," in the words of Perry Anderson or Gopal Guru. Like any nationalist notion of caste and untouchability, Nicholas Dirk's concept of

The stigma followed, and their voices drowned.
They yield the road to those of higher birth.
Their presence was marked by silence, not joy.
Yet, in their eyes, a fire still burns bright.
A spirit unbroken despite the plight.
For in the darkest corners, hope still gleams.
A dream of equality beyond extremes.
So let us heed their call, break down the wall,
That separates humanity, one and all.[40]
For until every soul is truly free,
We remain bound by our disgrace.
Let the village be a gathering place.
For every creed, every color, and every race.
And may the Untouchables no longer roam.
But they found their rightful place and were welcomed home.

"castes of mind" is limited and Janus-faced. Analysis is mine.

40. BAWS, vol. 3.

5. The Ladder Caste System

In the annals of history, a system is upheld,
Hinduism's Caste is a tale so cruelly spelled.
Brahmins at the peak, Kshatriyas next in line,
Vaishyas follow suit while Shudra toils in grime.
At the ladder's base, Untouchables bear the weight.[41]
Of oppression's chains, a destiny of hate.
A vertical hierarchy is where humanity has lost its way.
In the rigid confines of a caste system's cost.
Brahmins, the privileged, the chosen elite,
Presumed divine, their power is complete.
Kshatriyas, the warriors, bask in glory's hue.
While Vaishyas reap riches, a favored few.
Shudras,[42] the laborers, toil day and night.[43]
They ignore their sweat and blood, their plight out of sight.
And at the ladder's foot, Untouchables dwell,
Condemned to darkness, a living hell.
In the name of tradition, injustice prevails.
Untouchables' suffering impales their humanity.
A divinely decreed system
Yet, where is the divinity in this misery?
The ladder caste system is a blight on the land.
Where birth determines fate, where power's hand.

---

41. Mason, "Castle System of India," 648.

42. Shudras include the Gouda, Reddy, Kamma, Kapu, Velama, and other agricultural castes. They belong to the twice-born caste of foot troops. They can also be classified as non-Aryan or Anaryan races. Analysis is mine.

43. Mason, "Caste System of India," 648.

Few wield it at the expense of the many.
In the shadow of Caste, there's hardly any light.
But in the depths of despair, a whisper grows.
A cry for justice and a shift in the current situation
An outdated system, a relic of the past,
Where equality reigns, freedom is at last.
Untouchables are not lesser souls.[44]
Archaic roles do not define their worth.
In the tapestry of humanity, every thread holds worth.
No caste, no hierarchy, no birthright dearth.

---

44. Mason, "Caste System of India," 648.

6. Denied Access to the Hindu Spaces

In the hallowed halls of grand temples,
Untouchables stand barred, a cruel command.
Forbidden entry[45] to sacred ground,
Their presence was deemed impure in the Caste's tight bounds.
With bowed heads and hearts heavy,
Untouchables linger at gates so steadily.[46]
Their voices were silenced, and their spirits mourned.
As the temple's doors remain stubbornly drawn.
For centuries untold, this injustice prevails.[47]
As caste-based discrimination unfurls its sails,
Untouchables, deemed unworthy, shunned away,
Their prayers were unheard in the light of day.
But in the shadows, a flicker of hope
As Untouchables rise, refusing to cope.[48]
With resilience and courage, they demand their rights.
To worship freely in the temple's holy light.
For temples are not mere stone and mortar,
But sanctuaries of faith for every daughter and son.
Untouchables, too, seek solace and grace.
In divine embrace, in sacred space,
Their devotion is pure; their hearts are sincere,

---

45. Untouchables live in separate settlements located far away from Hindu localities. One example is the Madiga localities, where people who are considered impure or mobile dirt are prohibited from entering Hindu sacred and non-sacred localities even on auspicious occasions. Analysis is mine.

46. Mines, "Hindu Nationalism, Untouchable Reform," 59.

47. Mines, "Hindu Nationalism, Untouchable Reform," 61.

48. Mines, "Hindu Nationalism, Untouchable Reform," 62.

Yet Caste's cruel grip holds them in fear.[49]
Denied access to the divine's abode,
Untouchables tread paths long and wide.
But in the depths of their souls, a fire ignites.
A flame of defiance against the Caste's blights.
For they know their worth, their humanity is true,
And in their struggle, justice will prevail.
So let the temple bells ring, let the chants rise high,
As Untouchables reclaim what's rightfully nigh.
For in the temple's courtyards,
Caste has no place, only love.
Only grace, for every soul's embrace, exists.
Let the barriers crumble; let the gates swing wide.[50]
As Untouchables step forward with heads held high,
For in the eyes of the divine, all are one.
Together, we will break the hold of Caste.

---

49. Mines, "Hindu Nationalism, Untouchable Reform," 64.
50. Mines, "Hindu Nationalism, Untouchable Reform," 83.

7. Untouchables Should Not Sit in Front of Hindus

In the land where shadows dance with fear,
Untouchables tread with hearts austere.
Forbidden to sit among the blessed,
Their presence was cursed, and fate oppressed them.
Before the lofty, they dare not stand.
For death and shame await their hands.[51]
A girl, a woman, their mere presence ignites,
The fury of those who deem them blights.
Cast out from the light of religious grace,
They linger in the shadows, a marginalized race.
No seat at the table of the divine,
Their dignity was stolen, and their voices resigned.
In the eyes of the above, they are but filth.
A stain on the fabric of society's quilt.
To sit among them is a severe crime.
Punished with brutality, fueled by fear.[52]
Death lurks in the shadows, a silent threat.
For daring to defy the Caste's cruel set.
And as for the daughters of the untouchable clan,
The horror of gang rape is a vile plan.
Their bodies become battlegrounds of shame.
Society's blame crushed their spirits.
Yet, in the darkness, a flicker of hope,
A whisper of resistance is a way to cope.

51. United Nations, "Dalit."
52. United Nations, "Dalit."

For the Untouchables rise, their voices strong,
Against the injustice that has plagued them for a long time.
They demand equality, justice, and grace.
To reclaim their dignity and find their place.
No longer will they bow to the oppressor's might.
No longer will they cower in the night.[53]
For they are warriors, resilient, and bold.
Their stories of courage will be forever told.
So let us stand with them, hand in hand.
And fight for a world where all can stand.
Where Caste and creed hold no sway,
Dignity and respect pave the way.

---

53. United Nations, "Dalit."

8. Genocide against Untouchable Castes

In the heart of India's land, darkness spreads.
A genocide is silent, where humanity treads.
Untouchable castes, two hundred million strong.
Bound by chains of Caste, enduring for too long.
For centuries untold, the Caste's cruel decree,
Has condemned Untouchables to agony.
A genocide silent yet resounding loud,
Caste-based hatred is like a poisonous cloud.
From ancient times to the present day's light,
The plight of Untouchables is a constant fight.[54]
Invisible chains binding humanity's kin,
As Untouchables suffer beneath Caste's grim sin,
In fields, they toil under the scorching sun,
Yet Untouchables' battles are far from done.[55]
Caste-based oppression, an enduring crime,
A stain on the conscience, a shadow of time.
Two hundred million souls live in shadows.
Untouchability's genocide is a pervasive tide.
Struggling for breath in a prejudiced atmosphere,
Untouchables bear witness to an unfair world.
Yet, in the depths of despair, a whisper grows.[56]
A call for justice amidst Untouchables' woes.
For they are not lesser souls; their worth is not defined.
By archaic roles, by Caste's cruel bind.

    54. Barbara, "India's Untouchables."
    55. Barbara, "India's Untouchables."
    56. Barbara, "India's Untouchables."

So, let us rise against this caste-based creed.
Where privilege thrives and others bleed.
Let us break the chains and dismantle the Caste's hold.
And together, in unity, let us be bold.
Untouchables deserve dignity and grace.
Their place in society is not to be erased.[57]
Let us strive for equality; let justice prevail.
And untouchability's genocide, let us finally curtail.

---

57. Barbara, "India's Untouchables."

9. Religions and Their Genocide against Untouchables

In the annals of history, stained with blood,
Lie the tales of Untouchables, misunderstood.
Bound by Caste, oppressed by creed,
Their cries for justice were ignored, and their wounds still bleed.
Hinduism, with its ancient roots deep
Yet tainted by the sins of Caste, it keeps.
Untouchables were shunned, their voices silenced,
By Brahminical might, their hopes defied.
Muslims, too, with their call to prayer,
Yet she disregarded untouchable despair.
In the shadows of mosques, their plight is unknown.
Their dignity was shattered, and their dreams were overthrown.[58]
Buddhism, preaching compassion's creed,
Yet they failed to heed the untouchable need.[59]
For in the land of the Buddha's birth,
Their suffering is ignored, and their cries are unheard.
Jainism, with its vow of non-violence,
Yet complicit in the untouchable's silence.
For in the Caste hierarchy, they, too, played a part.
Their hands were stained with the untouchable's heart.
Sikhs, with their sword of justice drawn,
Yet they failed to protect the untouchable's dawn.
In the fields of Punjab, where sweat did flow,

---

58. Dube, *Untouchable Pasts*, 1790.
59. Dube, *Untouchable Pasts*, 1810.

Untouchables toiled; their humanity lay low.[60]
Parsees, with their fire burning brightly,
Yet turned away from the untouchable plight.
In the towers of silence, where the dead repose,
Untouchables' hopes withered like forgotten roses.
Each religion, with its divine claim,
Yet stained by the untouchable's pain.
In their quest for purity and grace,
Untouchables were left without a place.
But amidst the darkness, a ray of light,
Christianity stood, shining bright.
For in its embrace, Untouchables were found,
A sanctuary of love where hope abounds.[61]
So, let us remember the untouchable's plight.
And strive for a world where all have equal rights.
Where religion's cloak is torn apart,
And love and justice reign in every heart.

---

60. Dube, *Untouchable Pasts*, 1890.
61. Dube, *Untouchable Pasts*, 1895.

10. "Untouchable" under the "Brahmin" Peshwa Rule

Under the Peshwa's reign in Maharashtra's land,
Untouchables bore a great burden.
They were forced to tie pots to split their spit,[62]
And brooms to erase each footprint's writ.
In the alleys where silence reigned supreme,
Untouchables tread a marginalized team.
Their very presence was deemed unclean.
By Caste's cruel decree, a harsh regime.
With each step, they swept away,
Traces of their presence, come what may.
Their voices were hushed, forced to speak slowly.
In the Shadow of oppression's cruel blow.
Pot and broom, symbols of their plight,
Bound by the chains of a caste's cruel might.[63]
Their saliva, deemed impure and vile,
Their footprints were erased, mile by mile.
But in their hearts, a silent scream
of dignity lost in the Caste's dark scheme.
Their humanity was denied and scorned,
In the name of tradition, cruelty is adorned.
Yet amidst the darkness, a flicker of light,
The Untouchables' silent fight.[64]
For justice whispered in the winds,

---

62. Guru, "How Egalitarian," 5005.
63. Guru, "How Egalitarian," 5005.
64. Guru, "How Egalitarian," 5005.

They resisted oppression's binds.
Their resilience is a testament to true
To the human spirit, shining through.
For though the Peshwa's rule may have passed,
Their legacy is in history's grasp.
Let us remember their struggles boldly.
The tales of old are forever told.
And strive for a world where all are free.
From the chains of a caste's tyranny.

11. King Sayajirao Gaekwad III of Baroda: A Tale of Generosity toward Ambedkar

In the corridors of power, where monarchs reign,
A tale of generosity, devoid of stains.
Maharaja Gaekwad[65] of Baroda's name,
A beacon of hope in Ambedkar's fame.
He saw in Ambedkar a brilliant mind,
Untouched by Caste, humanity-inclined.[66]
So, he bestowed upon him a gift so grand,
A scholarship to traverse distant land.
To Colombia's halls, where knowledge soared,
And London's School of Economics was adored.
With dreams in his heart and vision clear,
Ambedkar embarked without fear.
But even amidst the halls of learning's grace,
Untouchability reared its ugly face.
From Hindu peons and clerks, an evil stare,
Mocking his dreams with a cruel glare.[67]
Yet undeterred, Ambedkar pressed on,
Through discrimination's darkness, he shone.
He knew that education was the key.
To unlock the chains of Caste and be free.
With each degree earned and each milestone passed,
His determination is forever steadfast.

---

65. Baroda King Sayajirao Gaekwad III granted a scholarship to Ambedkar in 1919 to pursue higher education in the western university.

66. Keer, *Life and Mission*.

67. Keer, *Life and Mission*.

Maharaja Gaekwad's gift—a guiding light,
Guiding Ambedkar through the darkest night.
For the Maharaja saw beyond the caste divide,
Recognized in Ambedkar is an undeniable spirit.
A scholar, a leader, destined for great things,
Empowered by knowledge, with wisdom's wings.
So, let us remember Maharaja Gaekwad's deed.
It is a noble act in a time of need.
For he saw in Ambedkar's potential untold,
And paved the way for a bold future.[68]
And let us honor Ambedkar's fight.
Against untouchability's blight.
For he rose above discrimination's snare,
And left a legacy beyond compare.

---

68. Keer, *Life and Mission*.

12. Philosopher Ambedkar: The Western Knowledge in Eastern Spaces

In the halls of knowledge, where wisdom reigns supreme,
A scholar emerged like a brilliant sparkle.
Ambedkar, with his vast and bright intellect,
He earned his PhD, a beacon of light.[69]
At Columbia University, across the sea,
He dove into politics with fiery determination.
Political science, his chosen field,
A passion ignited, and a future was revealed.
With London's School of Economics in sight,
He pursued economics with all his might.
The intricacies of wealth, poverty, and power
He captured his mind in that academic tower.
Through hours of study and nights long and deep,
He honed his mind and his resolve to keep.[70]
Ambedkar knew that with each degree earned,
He'd break down barriers with his lessons learned.
His journey was fraught with struggle and strife.
But through it all, he embraced life.
Education, he knew, was the key.
To unlock doors and set minds free.
With his PhDs in hand, he stood tall,
Ready to answer destiny's call.
To uphold the rights of the oppressed,
Create a future filled with blessings for everyone.

69. BAWS, 17:235.
70. BAWS, 7:238.

So, let us honor Ambedkar's legacy.
His academic prowess is a sight to see.
For in his pursuit of knowledge and truth,
He paved the way for a brighter youth.[71]
May his story inspire generations anew to seek education and pursue dreams.
For in the pursuit of wisdom's light,
lies the power to overcome every plight.

---

71. BAWS, 7:242.

13. Temple Entry Movement for Untouchables

In the heart of Bombay, at nineteen twenty-seven,
Ambedkar's voice rang like the toll of heaven.
At Thakurdwar temple, he made his stand,
Demanding justice with a righteous hand.
Untouchables barred from temples of faith,
They were denied their rights by the Caste's cruel wrath.
But Ambedkar rose, with courage untold,
To break down barriers and be bold.[72]
Through the streets of Poona, in nineteen twenty-nine,
Ambedkar marched, his resolve divine.
At Parvati temple, he fought the fight.
For equality's sake, amid the night.
But the doors remained shut against his plea.
Untouchability's grip refuses to let go.
Yet undeterred, Ambedkar pressed on,
His spirit was unbroken, and his hope was not gone.
In Nasik's Kalaram temple, in nineteen thirty,
Ambedkar stood tall, his heart still sturdy.[73]
With each agitation, he shook the ground.
Challenging tradition with a resounding sound.
But even amidst his democratic cries,
Support was lacking from liberal allies.
Leftists and nationalists looked the other way.
To Ambedkar's struggle, his earnest cry.[74]

72. BAWS, 5:125.
73. BAWS, 5:127.
74. BAWS, 5:131.

Even Gandhi, whom the Mahatma revered,
He denied his support as Untouchables neared.
For in the eyes of some, Caste held sway.
And the Untouchables were kept at bay.
But Ambedkar's fight did not wane.
His spirit was ablaze, like an eternal flame.
For he knew that justice, though slow to come,
Would one day prevail, like the rising sun?
So, let us remember Ambedkar's quest.
To open the doors and put the Caste to rest.
His legacy lives on in the fight for rights,
To break down barriers and bring forth light.

14. India's First Civil Rights Movement for Untouchable Women

In the land where rivers flow with history's tale,
Ambedkar stood, his voice a mighty gale.
In nineteen twenty-seven, in Mahad's embrace,
He led a satyagraha with dignity and grace.[75]
Untouchable women, oppressed for years,
Denied the right to shed their tears.
Their saris draped low, below the waist.
A symbol of the Caste's cruel embrace.
But Ambedkar fought with courage, strength,
To right the injustice, to correct the wrong.
For he believed in equality's flame,
And the dignity of every untouchable name.
Through Mahad's streets, they marched in stride.
Untouchable women, with hope as their guide.
Their saris were held high, above the waist.[76]
A symbol of freedom no longer debased.
But faced with resistance from those in power,
They stood their ground, hour after hour.[77]
For Ambedkar's vision, they dared to fight.
To reclaim their dignity in the face of spite.
With each step forward, they challenged the norm.
I am breaking the chains of tradition's storm.
Untouchable women's voices are strong.

75. BAWS, 17:54.
76. BAWS, 17:58.
77. BAWS, 17:86.

She refused to be silenced and declined to be wronged.
Though the road was long and the journey hard,
They held onto hope, their spirits unmarred.[78]
For they knew that change, though slow to come,
Would one day shine like the morning sun?
And so, they stood, in Mahad's light,
Untouchable women are reclaiming their rights.[79]
To wear their saris, as Hindu women do,
A symbol of freedom, a dream come true.
So let us remember Mahad's call:
And the courage of those who dared to stand tall.
Ambedkar's legacy will forever shine.
A beacon of hope in justice's design.

---

78. BAWS, 17:84.
79. BAWS, 17:111.

15. Mahad Movement for the Right to Drink Water

In the heart of Maharashtra, where history sings,
A tale of courage to spread its wings.
March 20, a day of defiance and might.
Mahad Satyagraha, in freedom's light.
Led by Ambedkar, with a clear vision,
Untouchables gathered without fear.
To claim their right to drink from the tank,
In Mahad's soil, their spirits rank.
For too long, they had been denied.
Access to water by Caste's cruel tide.
But on this day, they stood as one.
In the face of oppression, their battle has begun.
With determination etched on every face,
They marched forward in dignity's embrace.
To the public tank, they made their way.
They are demanding justice without delay.
But met with resistance from those in power,
Their voices echoed hour after hour.
For Ambedkar's vision, they fought the fight.[80]
To break down barriers and bring forth light.
In the scorching sun, they stood their ground.
Their resolve is unyielding, and their spirits are unbound.
They knew that water, a basic need,
Should not be tainted by a caste's cruel deed.[81]

80. BAWS, 17:42.
81. BAWS, 17:48.

With each step forward, they challenged the norm.
They are defying tradition's oppressive storm.
For Mahad Satyagraha, it was more than a plea.
It was a cry for justice for all to see.
And though the road was long and the journey hard,
They held onto hope, their spirits unmarred.
On this day, in Mahad's embrace,
Untouchables stood in freedom's grace.
So let us remember, on this sacred day,
The courage of those who led the way.
For Mahad Satyagraha, a beacon of light,
Guiding us forward in justice's fight.

16. Burning the Founding Father of Genocide against Untouchables: Manusmriti

In the flames of rebellion, in the heat of the night,
Ambedkar stood, his courage bright.
In December of twenty-seven, a fiery sight,
He burned the Manusmriti in a bold rite.
For too long, its pages dictated fate.
We are dividing humanity with a vicious hatred.
Pure and impure, its words decreed.
A hierarchy of castes for all to see.
However, Ambedkar, with righteous ire,
I refused to bow to the Caste's cruel fire.
In the heart of Maharashtra, in defiance's glow,
He lit the pyre to let Caste's chains go.
The Manu[82] smriti, a symbol of oppression's hand,
Its verses are like shackles across the land.
But Ambedkar's flames licked and leaped.[83]
It was burning away the chains that had been kept.
For he believed in equality's creed,
And the worth of every human seed.[84]

---

82. Every Hindu canonical law that directed the genocide against the Untouchable classes throughout time and place was written by the Brahmin Manu. All Brahmins are Manus. Manu is immortal. He or she is a live human being who, via non-Brahmin creatures like them, carries the ancient ideals. Throughout the depths of western areas, Manu is a person who became a Hindu through organizations like ISCON, Hare Rama, and others throughout Europe and other regions of the world. Analysis is mine.

83. BAWS, 17:67.

84. BAWS, 17:86.

No longer would Caste dictate destiny's course,
No longer would Untouchables bear their remorse.
As Manusmriti turned to ash and smoke,
Ambedkar's message rang clear, and he woke.[85]
No longer would they bow to the Caste's decree,
They were born free to live and to be.
In the echoes of that fiery night,
A new dawn emerged, shining bright.
A dawn of equality, justice, and grace.
Where all were seen in their rightful place.
So let us remember that in December's call,
Ambedkar's courage in standing tall.
For he dared to challenge, to ignite the flame,
And burn away Caste's dark claim.
In the ashes of manusmriti's blaze,
A new era dawned with brighter days.
For Ambedkar's fire, it burned so brightly.
They are illuminating the path to freedom's light.

---

85. BAWS, 17:91.

17. The Call For The Annihilation Of Caste

In the chambers of wisdom, where ideas take flight,
Ambedkar's voice is bold and bright.
He called for a revolution, a radical decree.
The annihilation of Caste,[86] to set minds free.
For too long, Caste had held sway.
Dictating lives, day by day.
But Ambedkar saw through its façade,[87]
A system of oppression is cruel and flawed.
With words like swords, he cut through the veil,
Exposing Caste's grip, its power frail.
He called for unity beyond the caste divide.
To break the chains and cast them aside.
In speeches and writings, he laid bare,
The injustices of Caste, the burdens to bear
He challenged tradition with every breath.
For the annihilation of Caste, he fought to the death.
He understood that without the destruction of Caste,
True equality could never be enjoyed.
He called for a society where birth didn't dictate,
A person's worth or their fate.

---

86. Ambedkar never gave up being a Hindu; he just converted to Buddhism. Another offshoot of Hinduism that has caste and untouchability ingrained in it is Buddhism. He consented to cremation, which strips someone of their human status and love. Cremation is the dishonorable act by which a dead person declares their inhumanity. Ambedakar lost his human status when he was cremated. The act of cremation is a violation of nonviolence, peace, humanity, love, and human status. Analysis is mine.

87. BAWS, 11:81.

His words resonated across the land.[88]
It is inspiring a movement to take a stand.
To dismantle Caste, brick by brick,
And build a future without its thick.
But the battle was long, the struggle steep,
The Caste's roots run deep.
Yet Ambedkar's vision gave us hope.[89]
To break free from the Caste's suffocating rope.
So, let us remember his call to arms.
To dismantle the Caste's cruel charms.
For until Caste is eradicated, we must fight.
To ensure equality's everlasting light.

---

88. BAWS, 11:87.
89. BAWS, 11:95.

18. The Ramsay Macdonald Award of 1932 for Untouchables

In the year thirty-two, a decree was made,
The Community Award, in justice's shade.
For untouchable castes, a ray of light,
Amidst the darkness of Caste's blight.
Amidst the tumult of the political fray,
It was a momentous decision to pave the way.
To grant Untouchables fair representation,
In the halls of power, to have a share.
For too long, they had been pushed aside.
They were denied their rights by the Caste's cruel tide.
But with the Community Award, a door was opened wide.
For Untouchables to step into the tide.
No longer relegated to the fringes of society's fold,
They were recognized, and their voices were bold.
Given seats reserved in legislative halls,
To represent their people and answer the calls.
Yet amidst the celebration, there lay strife.[90]
As voices rose in protest against the tide,
Opposition stirred from those entrenched in power,
Who feared the shift in Caste's ivory tower?
But Ambedkar stood firm, his vision clear.
To fight for justice without fear.
The Community Award was a step forward.[91]
In the struggle against Caste, there is a rallying chord.

---

90. Anderson, *Indian Ideology*, 40–41.
91. Anderson, *Indian Ideology*.

In the heart of the award lay a promise of bright,
Of fair representation and equal rights.
A recognition of Untouchables' worth,
A step towards justice is a step towards birth.
Though the road was long and the journey hard,
The Community Award stood like a guiding star.[92]
A beacon of hope in the fight for rights
For Untouchables to stand in freedom's light.
So let us remember the Community Award's decree:
And the promise it held was for equality.
Until we hear every voice and secure every right,
The struggle continues until justice is ensured.

---

92. Anderson, *Indian Ideology*.

19. Professor Dr. B. R. Ambedkar the Knowledge the Lived Experience with Humiliation

In the corridors of academia, where knowledge reigns supreme,
Two tales of resilience, like a haunting dream.
Ambedkar, with his brilliance, rose from an untouchable plight.
Two PhDs in hand, yet shunned in Hindu's sight.[93]
His intellect is unmatched, his spirit is strong and true,
Yet, despite the Caste's cruel chains, they were still trapped and slew.
In the land of his birth, discrimination's bitter sting,
A constant reminder of the pain that Caste can bring.
On distant shores, Jewish laureates faced their strife.
Rampant anti-Semitism, slicing like a knife.[94]
Bigotry's dark cloud overshadows their brilliance.
Yet, through the storm, their voices still rang loud.
But compare the two, and you'll find
Caste-based genocide leaves no soul behind.
For Ambedkar, despite his laurels and acclaim,
Faced with prejudice and hatred, his struggle was not in vain.
The Holocaust's horrors, yes, they were vast.
But caste-based genocide still holds fast.
Untouchables, downtrodden, denied their very worth,
The caste system's girth eclipsed their suffering.
October 7, a day of tragedy and pain,
Yet, for Untouchables, every day is the same.

---

93. Dewey, *Democracy and Education*.
94. Dewey, *Democracy and Education*.

Their lives were deemed expendable, their dignity stripped away,
The caste system forces them to stay.
So let us not forget, as we ponder history's page,
The untold suffering of those in the Caste's cruel cage.
Ambedkar's legacy, like a beacon in the night,
It shines a light on injustice and the fight for what is right.
In the face of caste-based genocide, let us stand,
Hand in hand, they united into a mighty band.[95]
Until every untouchable is genuinely free,
We cannot claim justice or equality.

---

95. Dewey, *Democracy and Education*.

20. Scavenging Caste: India's Sub-Human

In the shadows of Caste, where darkness dwells,
Lies a tale of oppression untold in its spells.
Scavenging Caste,[96] among Untouchables they roam,
Oppressing their own is a tragic syndrome.
Ambedkar was born to the dominant Mahar caste.[97]
Knew well the divisions that Caste's grip amassed.
Even among Untouchables, a hierarchy reigns.
A system of oppression that leaves deep stains.
The scavenging Caste works and strives.
But under the weight of Caste, they barely survive.
For Brahmin's design, to divide and to rule,
Leaves Untouchables trapped in a cruel duel.
Within their ranks, they're forced to obey.
The dictates of Caste, day after day.
Superior Untouchables, looking down with disdain,
On those deemed inferior in the Caste's cruel chain.
But Ambedkar, with his wisdom bright,
I saw through the Caste's veil its deceptive might.
He called for unity among the oppressed.
To break the chains and rise above.[98]
For every Caste, be it high or low,
Is but a pawn in Brahmin's cruel show?

---

96. The scavenger caste is Untouchable among Untouchable Castes. The fundamental tenet of Hindu doctrine is to subjugate and subjugate the untouchable. Analysis is mine.

97. Wankhede, "Human Dignity Argument," 109.

98. Wankhede, "Human Dignity Argument," 112.

Divide and conquer, the age-old plan,
To keep humanity enslaved by the Caste's cruel hand.
But Ambedkar's vision shines so clearly,
A future where caste divisions disappear.[99]
Where everyone is untouchable, no matter their Caste,
Stands equal and free from the shadows cast.
So, let us heed his call and break the chains.
Of the Caste's oppressive grip, where darkness reigns.
Until every untouchable is genuinely free, the Caste's legacy will remain.

---

99. Wankhede, "Human Dignity Argument," 116.

21. Sati: Where Wives Embraced the Funeral Pyre's Light

In the shadowed realms of ancient lore,
Where myths and legends freely soar,
There lies a tale of love entwined,
Yet bound by fate, cruelly designed.
Sati,[100] they called this tragic rite,[101]
Where wives embraced the funeral pyre's light,
Their souls aflame with devotion's fire,
Consumed in sorrow's funeral choir.
In temples and large villages,
Echoes of anguish, a mournful call,
Hindu wives, veiled in sorrow's shroud,
Bound by tradition, their fate was avowed.
The husband's death was a devastating blow.
But tradition demanded a greater woe.
For in the embers of his funeral pyre,
She, too, must burn with fervent desire.[102]
With tear-stained cheeks and a heavy heart,
She bids farewell, her world apart.
To join her love in realms unseen,
Where eternity's embrace shall gleam.

    100. In our times, Sati practices are common among Touchable or Sacred Castes. The Roop Kanwar case in Rajastan in 1987 is the most recent instance of Sati practice. Since state and nonstate actors are representatives of the ancient Sati practice and ideology, many Sati instances go unreported, undetected, and blatantly ignored. Analysis is mine.
    101. Gilmartin, "Sati, the Bride," 142.
    102. Gilmartin, "Sati, the Bride," 145.

Her sacrifice is a profound testament.
To love unyielding, forever bound,
Yet, in the flames, a silent scream
A tragedy veiled in tradition's gleam.
For those who can measure the depths of pain,
In hearts that break, yet love sustains.
As embers flicker and darkness falls,
A haunting echo is within the temple walls.[103]
But let us not forget the souls that weep.
In silent vigil, their sorrows steep,
For Sati, though revered in ancient lore,
Speaks of oppression always.
Let love not be a chain that binds.
But a gentle breeze that freedom finds
For every life, a sacred flame,
Unmarred by tradition's cruel game.
In the annals of time, let us inscribe,
A tale of love that does not prescribe
The sacrifice of souls on pyres is bright.
But it is a journey of love in endless flight.

---

103. Gilmartin, "Sati, the Bride," 152.

22. The Land Where Hindu and Islamic Hearts Unite

In the quiet corners of tradition's embrace,
Where echoes of ancient norms still hold their place,
There is a tale of unions deemed taboo.
Where views shadow love's path,[104]
In the heartlands, where Hindu and Islamic customs collide,
Lies the practice of marrying blood cousins side by side.
A practice[105] born of tradition's firm grip,
But beneath its surface lies a truth too grim to skip.
For within the veins of blood that intertwine,
Lie echoes of a past that refuses to align.
Where the shadows of kin taint love's bloom,
And the whispers of taboo danced in the wind.
In the name of tradition, they forge their bonds.
But beneath the surface, a silent cry responds.
For love entwined with blood, is it love at all?
Or are they the shackles of tradition, holding hearts in thrall?
In the eyes of society, they may find acceptance.
But in the depths of their souls lies a silent lament.
For to love within blood's circle is to court a fate,
Where whispers of judgment forever dictate.
So let us heed the call of hearts yearning to be free.
And break the chains of tradition that are bound by cruelty.

104. BAWS, 3:230.

105. Across the world or anywhere there are followers of Hindu, Islamic, Jain, Sikh, Buddhist, or Parse beliefs, cross-cousin marriages or same-blood marriages are deeply ingrained.

For love knows no bounds, nor do the dictates of kin.
It thrives in the freedom where true love can begin.

23. Traditional Marriage System: No Choice to Make, No Freedom to Rejoice

In the shadows of tradition's veil,
A story unfolds—a heart-wrenching tale.
Where Hindu daughters, in silence, wait,[106]
Bound by the chains of an unjust fate.
Arranged as they are, without a voice,
There's no choice to make, no freedom to rejoice.
Forced into unions with age's embrace,
Their autonomy was lost without a trace.
In the annals of time, this practice endures.
A culture entrenched, where silence obscures,
The cries of women, oppressed and bound,
In marriages[107] dictated, their voices drowned.
Older men come with greedy eyes.
To claim young brides is a cruel disguise.
Their innocence was stolen, their dreams denied,
Tradition casts them aside.
What is consent in this cruel charade?
Where women are bartered, and fortunes are made,
Their bodies traded like goods for sale.[108]
In a system where patriarchy prevails.
No regard for their wishes, their hopes, or their fears
There is no consideration for their silent tears,
Forced into roles they never chose,

---

106. BAWS, 14:3.
107. Arranged marriages are prisons on earth. Analysis is mine.
108. BAWS, 14:60.

Their dignity was shattered, and their spirits were enclosed.
But let us not falter; let us not forget.
The power of voices that rise and fret is profound.
For in the echoes of resistance vital,
We find the courage to right the wrong.
Let us dismantle this culture of rape.
Where women's lives are mere landscapes,[109]
Let us stand in solidarity, hand in hand.
And reclaim the rights that they demand.
Every woman deserves to have her voice heard.
Every injustice requires the stirring of a truth.
In the struggle for justice, we shall prevail.
And break the chains of this oppressive tale.

---

109. BAWS, 14:61.

24. Dowry Demands Innocent Lives

In the web of Dowry's tangled thread,
Their dreams entwined, their hopes misled,
Forced to bear the burden of tradition's weight,
Where daughters are but objects of fate,
In the alleys where poverty thrives,
Dowry[110] demands innocent lives,[111]
Parents, they toil, their meager wealth,
To buy their daughters' fleeting stealth.
In the eyes of society's disdain,
Untouchable's struggle, their efforts in vain,
For dowry culture, a relentless vice,
Casts its shadow, a cruel device.
Young brides, they tremble, hearts torn,
As dowry demands leave them desolate,
Their worth is measured in material gain.
Their dignity was lost in tradition's chain.
But who shall speak for the voiceless cries?
Of daughters sold beneath darkened skies?
Oppressive hands crushed their dreams.[112]
Their futures were shackled in desolate lands.
The dowry culture bears a deep stain.
Where brides are sold like herded sheep,
Untouchables bear the brunt of its sting.

---

110. The cruel custom of dowries is well ingrained in Asian, African, and other cultures. Analysis is mine.
111. Teays, "Burning Bride," 30.
112. Teays, "Burning Bride," 34.

Their suffering echoed in silence's ring.
However, amid despair's cruel might,
A glimmer of hope, a flickering light
For voices to rise in courage and boldness,
To challenge the norms that have long been controlled.
Let us unravel the chains that bind.
Let justice reign; let compassion find
Every daughter has a bright future.
Dowry's shadow fades from sight.[113]
In the heartland where Caste divides,
Let love and equality be our guides.

---

113. Teays, "Burning Bride," 36.

25. "Madiga" Devadasis Forced into the Temple Prostitution

In the temples where shadows dance,
A darkened tale of circumstance,
Devadasis, daughters of the untouchable Caste,[114]
Bound to serve, their freedom was surpassed.
Forced into the roles of temple dancers,
Their innocence was stolen, their bodies laid bare,
To satisfy the desires of Brahmin's decree,
And non-Brahmin Hindus, their lust set free.
In the sanctum, where gods are revered,
Untouchable daughters,[115] their fate steered,
To serve as vessels for others' pleasure,
Their cries were unheard, a silent measure.
Caste-based massacres stain the land.
Blood-soaked soil beneath a tyrant's hand
Untouchables were slaughtered, their lives forsaken,
Their dignity was shattered, and their spirits were shaken.[116]
Gang rapes echo through the night.
As darkness descends, obscuring light,
Untouchable women, their bodies defiled,
By those who wield power, by those who've compiled.
In the annals of history, their stories are told.
Of atrocities committed, of horrors unfolding,

---

114. Jangam, *Dalits*.

115. In Asian social patterns, Touchable Castes force their Devadasi culture over Untouchable Castes. Analysis is mine.

116. Jangam, *Dalits*.

Yet justice eludes, like a distant dream,
For those deemed lesser in society's scheme.
But let not their cries be lost in vain.
Let their suffering not be met with disdain.
For in their struggle, a flame ignites.
A beacon of hope amid endless nights.[117]
Let us confront the demons of Caste,
Let us shatter the chains of the past,
For every life lost, every soul scarred,
demands justice's sword, swift and brutal.
In the temples where shadows dance,
Let freedom reign, let love enhance,
For Devadasis, untouchable daughters are fair.
They deserve dignity beyond compare.

---

117. Jangam, *Dalits*.

26. Kanchikacherla Kotesu "Madiga" Massacre

In the heart of Andhra Pradesh, in Kanchikacherla's quiet embrace,
It tells a tale of horror, Caste, and love's disgrace.
Kotesh, a son of Madiga, knew no divide,
But Caste denied the truth of love.
In the shadows of prejudice, he dared to love a Kamma maiden.[118]
But in the eyes of society, this was a sin too heavy to bear.
For centuries, bound by the chains of tradition's cruel decree,
Untouchables and Kammas,[119] never to intercede.
Yet love, like a wildflower, knows no boundaries nor chains.
It blooms in the hearts of the oppressed amidst sorrow's rains.
But the flames of hatred, fueled by the Caste's cruel hand,
Turned love's sweet melody into a dirge across the land.
With malice in their hearts, the oppressors struck their blow.
In the daylight, they laid Kotesh low.
With Kerosene's cruel embrace, they set his spirit alight.
A sacrifice to their Caste in the shadows of the night.
As flames consumed his flesh, his cries pierced the silent air.
But the deafening roar of Caste drowned out his despair.
And as he fell into darkness, his spirit soared above.
A martyr for love's cause, in the arms of eternal love.
But his story does not end in the ashes of despair.
His sacrifice ignited a flame. A cry for justice is rare.
In the annals of history, his name shall forever shine.

---

118. Daaham, "Kanchikacherla Massacre."

119. The foot soldiers of the twice-born castes, namely Kamma, Reddy, Kapu, Velama, Gouda, Yadav, and others, have been instructed by Hindu scriptures to punish Untouchables for breaking the laws of purity and impurity.

A beacon of hope in a world where Caste confines.
So let us remember Kotesh, his love, his pain, his plight,
And vow to fight against Caste with all our strength and might.

27. 1985 Karamchedu Carnage: The Genocide Unfolded

In the fields of Karamchedu, where the crops once grew tall,
Lies a tale of horror in which innocence did fall.
With agricultural iron tools wielded by hands of hate,
The Kamma caste Hindus sealed their victims' fate.
Madiga Untouchables, deemed lower than low,
In the eyes of their oppressors, they are mere targets in the row.
Driven by caste pride and fueled by bigotry's flame,[120]
They unleashed their fury, and terror became their name.
Ten thousand strong, they descended like a storm.
In the peaceful village, where screams were the norm,
Innocent lives shattered by the cruelty of Caste,
As blood stained the soil, the heavens looked aghast.
Madiga children, girls, and women bore the brunt of their wrath.
As the horror of their fate echoed along the path,
Gang-raped and violated, their dignity torn asunder,
In the wake of the massacre, their cries rent the thunder.
Untouchable houses burned, their livelihoods destroyed,[121]
While cattle lay slaughtered in a scene devoid of joy,
Hundreds were left maimed, physically scarred for life,
By the savagery unleashed amidst the caste-driven strife.
But in the face of darkness, there still flickers a light.
A beacon of hope amidst the endless night.
For the souls of the fallen, cry out for justice to be true.[122]

---

120. Berg, "Karamchedu," 385.
121. Berg, "Karamchedu," 387.
122. Berg, "Karamchedu," 380.

To heal the wounds of Karamchedu and break the Caste's brutal hue.
So let us remember the victims, their stories untold.
And vow to fight injustice with brave and bold hearts.
For in the face of hatred, love shall always prevail.
And the echoes of their suffering will never grow stale.

28. 1997 Ramabai Killings: Injustice Reigned in a Ruthless Display

In Mumbai's heart, where dreams unfold,
It is a tale of tragedy, grim and cold.
In Rama Bai's colony, on that fateful day,
Injustice reigned in a ruthless display.
A statue defiled, a symbol of pride,
B. R. Ambedkar's legacy cast aside,[123]
Dalit voices rose in peaceful protest,
But it was met with violence that was unjust and grotesque.
On July 11, 1997, the streets did cry.
As shots rang out, piercing the sky,
Ten lives were lost in a relentless hail of bullets.
Their blood was staining the ground—a tragic pool.
Among the fallen, an innocent soul,
Caught in the crossfire, beyond control.
A bystander, not part of the fray,
Yet claimed by violence in the chaos' sway.
Later, the police, with batons raised high,
Unleashing their fury with a brutal cry,
Lathi charge upon lathi charge, without restraint,
Leaving bodies bruised and hearts heavy with lament.
Caste-based prejudice, an evil seed,
In the hearts of those who choose to listen,
Leaders tainted by discrimination's stain,
Whose actions bring forth anguish and pain?
But in the aftermath of this dark hour,

---

123. BAWS, 17:345.

A chorus of voices rose with power.
Demanding justice for the lives unjustly taken,[124]
For the wounds inflicted, hearts shattered and forsaken.
Let us not forget the souls laid low.
In Rama bai's colony, where anguish did grow,
Their memory is a beacon, shining bright.
Guiding us towards truth and what is right.
May their sacrifice not be in vain.
As we strive to break a caste's cruel chain,
For in the heart of Mumbai and beyond,
We promise to persevere until we achieve justice.

---

124. BAWS, 17:351.

29. Khairlanji: The Horror of September 29, 2006

The heart of Maharashtra, in Khairlanji's embrace,
A massacre unfolded, leaving a scar in its trace.
On September 29, 2006, horror reigned supreme.
The Bhotmange family faced a nightmarish dream.
From the Mahar community, they hailed with pride,
However, the Maratha Kunbi received an unfair denial.[125]
A mob's brutal rage snuffs out four lives.
In a display of the Caste's vile, unforgiving cage.
Stripped naked, paraded in humiliation's cruel light,
Their dignity shattered, their plight a harrowing sight,
Sons were forced to watch as their mother and sister were defiled.
Their screams drowned in hatred and violence.
Refusing to obey, surrendering to hate's decree,
Their genitals were mutilated, their fate sealed cruelly,
Then, cast into oblivion, their bodies left to drown,
As the waters of injustice claimed what hatred had thrown,
Those meant to protect ignore a cry for help.
As justice faltered, leaving Dalits to reflect,
Considering the systemic biases and the caste-based divide,
That led to the massacre, where humanity died.
After two days of delay in the search for the slain,
As anguish and grief swept like torrential rain,
In the canal's depths, their bodies were found.
However, much of the evidence needs to be contaminated and unsound.

125. Teltumbde, *Persistence of Caste*.

Protests erupted, demanding justice be served.
Dalits resisted having their voices misconstrued.
Allegations of cover-ups, political sway,
This led to the case being handed to the CBI, they say.
Yet scars remain, etched in the land's very soul.
A reminder of the atrocities, the toll of Caste's cruel role.
In Khairlanji's tragedy, we find a call to fight.
In a world where justice reigns and all are treated right.

30. Agony of My Mother, Suguna Yadav: Love without Borders Is to Let Love Decree

In the fields of Yadav, Suguna arose.
A maiden of courage, her spirit composed,
She was bound by tradition, but her heart was free.
To love without borders is to let love decree.
Her eyes met Madiga, an untouchable son.[126]
Their love is forbidden, their union is undone,
Yet Suguna dared; she defied the divide.
Love knows no caste, no societal guide.
Fleeing the wrath of the orthodox few,
Her love in tow, her courage in view,
They sought refuge in the shadows and at night.
Two souls intertwined in love's resolute light.
Never again would she tread on her past,
Fear gripped her heart—fear that would last.
Her children, her treasures, her reason to fight,
She shielded them fiercely, with love's sacred might.
But tragedy struck—a blow so severe,

---

126. Titus Mattimalla, my father, is a Christian from Madiga who comes from an Untouchable Caste background. He also goes by Anand Mattimalla. He was loved by my mother, Patnala Suguna Yadav, also called Mattimalla Suguna Madiga, who married my father, Madiga. In the colonial era of the South Indian state of Andhra, my father's forefather, Matthew Miller, was a Finnish Protestant Christian missionary. He married my Madiga, an untouchable foremother, 250 years ago. My mother endured social marginalization and social boycott from her caste, village, parents, and relatives as a result of her marriage to my Untouchable father. Finally, my mother's firstborn, eight-years-old son, my elder brother Vijay was cruelly killed. It was a honor killing. This is our family history.

Her firstborn lost, in the shadows of fear,
For superstitions reigned, unquestioning beliefs held sway,
Tearing her world in darkness's array.
Untouchable they called, yet untouchable love,
Suguna's devotion, like the stars above,
Her sacrifice is a testament to her
To love's unyielding power; to love that grew.
In the heart of Suguna, a flame still burns brightly.
A mother's love, a guiding light,
She dared to defy and to love without fear.
A legacy of courage for all to revere.
In the annals of time, her story will stand.
A beacon of hope in a divided land,
For love knows no bounds, no caste,
no creed. In Suguna's embrace, all find reprieve.

31. My "Moonflower": Victim of Honor Killing

In the shadowed depths of grief and pain,
a tale of loss, a heart's refrain,
For an unnamed flowermoon, taken too soon,
By the hands of hate, beneath the moon.
In the womb of his/her mother, a life once bloomed,
A future untold, with dreams entombed,
But in the twisted web of Caste's cruel fate,
His/her breath was stolen, his/her voice silenced, of late.
Born into a love that knew no bounds,[127]
Yet, on India's soil, hatred abounds.
For an untouchable's love, a crime to some,
A forbidden union, where hope succumbs.
Your mother, a Hindu-Kapu maiden,[128]
Bound by ties of Caste, love dared to dare.
But her kin, blinded by prejudice's blight,
I needed to extinguish love's guiding light.
They kidnapped her, they plotted, they schemed,
Their hearts were consumed by hatred, it seemed.
And in their cruelty, they took a life.
Your innocent soul amidst the strife.
I did not know if you were a daughter or a son.
But in my heart, your presence has begun.
A beacon of hope in a world so dark,
Now lost forever, hatred's stark.

---

127. I have no idea if my child is a boy or a girl. The infant in question is the author of this book's son or daughter.

128. Mamidi Richa.

I escaped the fate they had planned for me.
A narrow brush with death's decree,
But you, my child, were not so blessed.
Taken from me, laid to rest.
In the eyes of those who sought to erase,
Our love, our bond, our sacred place.
I see the reflection of a society's shame.
Where Caste divides and love's flame.
But in your memory, I find resolve.
To challenge the norms that seek to dissolve,
The beauty of love, in its purest form,
For in love's embrace lies hope reborn.
Even though we took you before you were ready,
In my heart, you'll forever shine.
My unnamed son/daughter, in your absence, I'll fight.
For a world where love conquers hate's blight.

32. My "Flowermoon" Stanford: A Life Taken by Neo-Nazi Doctor

In the heart of "Holocaust" Germany's land, so unfair,
This is a tale of tragedy, a rare injustice.
Where shadows of prejudice cruelly unfold,
A father's anguish, a story untold.
In the embrace of his African bride,[129]
A love that bloomed, a bond so wide,
But amidst the joy, a darkness crept nearby.
A life was taken by ignorance and fear.
June's warmth bore witness to a crime.
A doctor's hand,[130] a heinous chime,
Forced vaccination,[131] against all rhyme,
A mother's womb is a sacred shrine.
On July's eve, young Stanford came,

---

129. Selamawit Hailu Bezabih, the Ethiopian Tigrayan.

130. At least two African women seeking asylum related their suffering at losing their children following vaccinations at the asylum offices. After receiving a vaccination, a woman of color from Ethiopia lost her twins. In an asylum camp, four children—including my son Stanford—died following vaccination. Despite the fact that some vaccines cannot be given to pregnant women, one or two German doctors are testing their shots on pregnant women of color who are seeking refuge. The majority of women who were seeking refuge were afraid to file any police complaints against a German gynecologist for fear of having their requests denied or being deported. We had casual conversations with them, during which they informed me and my Tigrayan wife of this.

131. On June 28, 2023, in the Bajuwarenstr, 1A refugee camp, Regensburg, a German gynecologist administered a vaccination to my African-Ethiopian-Tigray wife, "Selamawit Hailu Bezabih" Repevax. This vaccination caused my son, Stanford Suryaraju Mattimalla, to die on July 2 or 3, 2023.

His future is bright; his spirit is aflame,
But fate's cruel hand dealt its blow,
A life was snatched away in one cruel throw.
In the land of "racist" Germany, where justice[132] should reign!
A father's cry echoes, a heart in pain,
For race should not dictate life's decree,
Yet bigotry's poison still runs free.
A son lost to senseless bigotry's reign,
His innocence was robbed, his legacy stained,
But in the depths of sorrow, a plea rings clear:
For justice to rise, to wipe every tear.
In memory of Stanford, a soul so dear,
May his story ignite change and dispel every fear.
No race should suffer such a fate.
Injustice must fall before it's too late.

---

132. After telling us that my son's death was natural, German police dismissed the case without looking into our allegations of widespread racism and vaccination trials on pregnant women of color in asylum clinics. It's possible that a large number of colored moms lost their babies. We fled Ethiopia and India to the Czech Republic, where we encountered racial persecution on both a physical and psychological level from both state and nonstate actors. I was also prevented from purchasing food by numerous stores, including Tesco and Penny, stating that Black people are not permitted. I was battered by a bunch of locals in front of the Czech police. When I asked for assistance from the police, they grinned. We escaped to Germany from the Czech Republic to save our children where bigotry claimed the life of our son Stanford.

33. Echoes of "Untouchable" Girl's

In the shadows of history, a haunting refrain
Echoes of a "Untouchable" girl's anguish and pain.
Her innocence was stolen, her voice silenced, and she lost
A brutal assault at an unfathomable cost.
Across the ages, her story unfolds.
A narrative etched in the annals of the past.
In the heart of darkness, where justice failed,
A Dalit girl's dignity was brutally assailed.[133]
From the fields of oppression to the corridors of power,
Her plight remains constant, hour after hour.
Her body, a battleground where demons reign,
A victim of Caste, of society's disdain.
In the pages of time, her tale is told.
A reminder of the cruelty of hearts grown cold.
From ancient kingdoms to modern-day streets,
With the echoes of her suffering, the world still meets.[134]
In the shadow of Bhima Koregaon's battle,
Where valor clashed, and hope took flight,
An untouchable girl, a victim of despair,
Her silent screams linger in the air.
Lawmaking takes place in the halls of power.
An untouchable girl's justice is too often delayed.
Her tears[135] were ignored, her cries unheard.

---

133. Diwakar, "Sex as a Weapon," 122.
134. Diwakar, "Sex as a Weapon," 126.
135. In every Hindu hamlet, there occurs a rape of an Untouchable girl. Analysis is mine.

A casualty of a society, deeply absurd.
But in the face of darkness, a flicker of light
A beacon of hope in the depths of night.
For her story ignites a fire, a call to action,
To break the chains of oppression
with compassion. So, let us stand together in solidarity.
To fight for justice and equality. For every Untouchable girl.[136]
Someone has stolen their voice,
Let us rise as one, their dignity unshaken.
For in the heart of humanity, there lies a choice.
To listen, to act, to lend our voice.
To ensure that no Untouchable girl ever again,
Suffers the horror of such unspeakable pain.

---

136. Diwakar, "Sex as a Weapon," 130.

34. Forcing Untouchable Men to Consume the World's Foul Swirl

In the heartland, where shadows dance with shame,
It is a tale of horror, a blight on humanity's name,
Seven were arrested, their deeds unfurled,
Forcing Untouchable men to consume the world's foul swirl.[137]
Houses demolished, dreams torn asunder,
A grotesque spectacle, a nation's thunder,
Echoes of oppression, centuries old,
In the stench of hatred, truth stands bold.
Untouchable men, sons of a lesser god,
Targeted by tyrants, under oppression's rod,
Their dignity was trampled, their spirits scarred,
Yet in their resilience, hope's flame barred.
Forced to ingest the vilest waste,
Their humanity was questioned in this darkened haste.
But in their eyes, a silent defiance
Against the chains of the Caste's cruel alliance.
Arrested they were, justice's hand,
Yet scars remain across the land,
Homes razed to the ground, symbols of despair.
But in their rubble, cries for justice flare.
In the silence of agony, a nation's shame,
Echoes through history, bearing the same,
For oppression persists in myriad guises,[138]
But in unity's embrace, freedom shall rise.

---

137. Hanchinamani, "Human Rights Abuses," 6.
138. Hanchinamani, "Human Rights Abuses," 9.

Let not their suffering be in vain.
Their voices echo a relentless refrain.
In their plight, we find our call.
To break the chains, to stand tall.

35. Influence of Western Philosophers on Ambedkar

In the corridors of intellect, where ideas converge and flow,
Dr. Ambedkar sought enlightenment amidst prejudice's cruel throes.
Amidst the echoes of inequality, where Caste held sway,
He turned to Western philosophers to light his righteous way.
Bertrand Russell, with his rational mind and piercing gaze,[139]
Cast a beacon of reason through Ambedkar's troubled maze.
With logic as his guide and skepticism as his creed,
Ambedkar found, in Russell's words, the courage to proceed.
From the depths of Russell's works, where reason takes its flight,
Ambedkar gleaned a vision of justice shining brightly.
In the pursuit of truth and reason, he found his steadfast creed,
A beacon in the darkness for those in desperate need.
Through Russell's critique of power and advocacy for peace,
Ambedkar found a resonance with his quest for release.
For in the face of oppression and the weight of Caste's division,
Russell's ideals of liberty became Ambedkar's guide.
With each word penned by Russell, a seed of change was sown.
In Ambedkar's heart, it blossomed—a vision all his own.
For in the fusion of Eastern struggles with Western thought's embrace,
Ambedkar forged a legacy of dignity and grace.

So let us remember Ambedkar, not just as a bold leader,[140]
But as a scholar, drawing wisdom from thinkers of old,

---

139. Bertrand, "Principles of Social Reconstruction," in *Source Material on Dr. Babasaheb Ambedkar and the Movement of Untouchables*, 249–51.

140. Bertrand, "Principles of Social Reconstruction," in *Source Material on Dr. Babasaheb Ambedkar and the Movement of Untouchables*, 249–51.

For in the echoes of Russell's words, his influence is evident.
It is a testament to the power of ideas to banish doubt and fear.

36. Threads of Humiliation

In the tapestry of human existence, woven deep,
Lie threads of humiliation, where sorrows seep,
In the West's embrace, race becomes the wielder's rod.
Casting shadows of prejudice, a heavy, burdensome clod.[141]
The color of one's skin, a marker of shame or pride,
Defines paths of privilege, where prejudice resides,
In the West's gaze, discrimination's cruel hand,
Leaves scars of humiliation across the land.
But turn to the east, where Caste's cruel decree,
Defines Untouchables, in chains unfree,
Untouchability, a notion ancient and cruel,
A barrier to humanity, a twisted, damning fuel.
Denied the touch, the gaze, the simple right,
Untouchables bear the weight of society's blight.
Humiliation is woven into their daily strife.
A reminder of their place in the hierarchy's knife.
From the depths of humiliation's bitter cup,
Untouchables rise, refusing to be shut up.
Their voices, though silenced, echo loud and clear.
In the fight for dignity and justice, they steer.
For humiliation knows no boundaries, no race,
It's the shadow that darkens every space.
But in the face of adversity, resilience stands tall.[142]
A testament to the human spirit's call.
So let us not forget, in the West or the East,

141. Guru, *Humiliation*, 1–238.
142. Guru, *Humiliation*, 1–238.

The wounds of humiliation, the pain unleashed,
And strive for a world where dignity reigns.
Where equality's light forever sustains.

37. Equality in the Writings of Western Philosophers: Rousseau, Kant, Hegel, and Smith

In the corridors of thought, where Western minds did soar,
Rousseau, Kant, Hegel, and Smith, their voices bore,[143]
For recognition, respect, and dignity, they cried,
Against humiliation's[144] tide, they fiercely defied.
Rousseau, in his social contract, proclaimed,
Each soul's worth must be named.
For in the bonds of society, no one should be oppressed.
Every individual's dignity is to be confessed.
Kant, with his categorical imperative, stern and clear,
Demanded that each person's worth be held dear,
For in treating others as ends, never mere means,
Lies the essence of humanity's noblest scenes.
Hegel, in his dialectic dance, sought to unfold
The spirit's journey, where truth is told,
For in recognizing each other's humanity,
Lies the path to genuine community.

---

143. Guru, *Humiliation*, 2–3.

144. Even in places like Nagaland, where the Naga people uphold strict caste and untouchability laws against Untouchable Castes despite not being a caste themselves, Untouchables continue to face persecution. The Sema Naga "Scato Swu" family in Dimapur physically assaulted, degraded, and dehumanized me for loving their daughter twenty years ago. They had beaten me with iron rods and chains and said, "Dalit bastard, how dare you to love our Naga girl?" in front of hundreds of people, humiliating me. My clothing was taken off, and my nude body was captured on camera. Throughout time and place, humiliation of Untouchable Castes is a common occurrence. Even in Naga communities where Christianity is the primary religion, the caste system has permeated the community. It is my personal experience with Scato Swu family.

Smith, in the market's invisible hand, saw,
The importance of respect, without flaw,
For in every exchange, in every trade,
Dignity preserved must never fade.
Now, let us localize these Western ideals boldly.
In the struggles of Untouchables, untold,
In the caste-based societies they reside in,
Recognition, respect, and dignity are denied.
Against humiliation's onslaught, they raise their voice,[145]
Seeking recognition, a fundamental choice,
For they are not mere subjects of scorn.
But humans deserving of honor are newly born.
In the face of shame, degradation's sting,
They demand respect, equality, and
For in their voices and their cries,
Like the echoes of Western philosophy's wisdom.
So let us heed their call, their plea,
In terms of recognition, respect, and dignity,
And in their struggle, may we find
A world where humanity's light shines.

---

145. Guru, *Humiliation*, 313.

38. Humiliation, Violence, and Degradation between Jews and Untouchables

In the annals of history, where shadows loom,
Lie tales of shared sorrow, in silent gloom,
For Jews and Untouchables, both have known,
The bitter taste of humiliation's stone.
From the horrors of the Holocaust's dark abyss,
To Untouchables' plight, in Caste's cruel kiss,
Shared humiliation, a bond so deep,
In the depths of injustice, their sorrows seep.
Anti-Semitism's venom, a poison spread wide,
Jews were persecuted, their dignity denied,
Forced into ghettos, with violence and scorn,[146]
Their cries for recognition are endlessly borne.
Yet Untouchables, too, in India's land,
Know the weight of Caste's heavy hand,
Denied the touch, the gaze, the respect,
Under an oppressive system, they must deflect.
October 7, a day stained red,
Untouchables were massacred; their bodies bled.
In the name of Caste, violence was unleashed,
Their dignity was shattered, and their cries were released.
But while the Holocaust's horror is widely known,
Untouchables' suffering is often left alone.
Their shared humiliation, too often ignored,
Silence's sword compounds injustice.[147]

---

146. Landry et al., "Dehumanization and Mass Violence."
147. Landry et al., "Dehumanization and Mass Violence."

For untouchability's stain, like a festering sore,
It runs deep into the fabric of India's core,
Worse than the Holocaust.
In its insidious grip, Untouchables remain.
May their stories ignite a flame of change.
Injustice dismantled, across every range,
In recognizing their shared plight,
Loses hope for a world bathed in light.

39. Janus-Faced Hindus

In the annals of India's fight for freedom,
A tale of contradictions, we seldom deem,
For a while, Hindus battled colonial chains,
Within their ranks, injustice remains.
Janus-faced Hindus, with voices raised,[148]
Against the oppressor, their banners blazed.
Gandhi, Tilak, Nehru, and Tagore's names,
Echo through history, heralding fame.
Yet, in the shadows of their nationalist pride,
Caste's dark specter, they sought to hide.
Untouchables, shunned, marginalized, scorned,
Their cries for justice were cruelly ignored.
Bankim Chandra Chattopadhyay's[149] pen may write,
Of Mother India's glory, in the dawn's first light,
But in his silence, Caste's grip tightens.[150]
Untouchables' plight is forever frightening.
Gandhi's call for Satyagraha's might,
Rings hollow to those in Caste's night.
For a while, he championed India's cause,
Untouchables' suffering gave him pause.
Tilak's fiery words, like a beacon's flame,
Inspired millions in freedom's name,
But in his heart, Caste's shadows loomed.
Untouchables' dreams are forever doomed.

148. Aloysius, *Nationalism without a Nation*, 1–262.
149. Guru, *Humiliation*, 3–4.
150. Guru, *Humiliation*.

Nehru's vision of a modern state
Stood in stark contrast to the Caste's cruel fate,
Yet his actions belied his noble words.
Untouchables' cries still went unheard.
Tagore's verses, like melodies divine,
Spoke of unity in a land enshrined,
But in his silence, Caste's grip tightened.
Untouchables' dreams, forever frightened.
Janus-faced Hindus, in freedom's guise,
Their contradictions are a painful surprise.
While they fought the foreign yoke,
Untouchables' chains never broke.[151]
Let us remember their dual faces.
In the annals of India's race,
For true freedom lies in equality's light,
Where Caste's dark shadows take flight.

---

151. Guru, *Humiliation*.

40. Untouchable Philosophers: Ambedkar and Gopal Guru the Semi-Theoretical Lights

In the realm of thought, where ideas intertwine,
Untouchable theorists Ambedkar and Gopal Guru[152] shine,
Their works, like beacons in the night,
Illuminate the path to justice's light.
Ambedkar, with wisdom, fierce, and bold,[153]
Championed equality in a caste-bound world,
His vision, like Rousseau's social contract, is clear.
Called for recognition, dignity is near.
Kant's categorical imperative, Ambedkar's guide,
Demanded respect for each soul's stride,
For in treating all as ends, never mere means,
Lies the essence of humanity's noblest scenes.
Hegel's dialectic dance, Ambedkar knew,
For in struggle's embrace, truths accrue.
In the journey towards recognition's shore,
Untouchables' dignity, always.
Adam Smith, with his market's invisible hand,
I saw the importance of dignity's stand,
For in every exchange, in every trade,
Human worth must never fade.
Marx, with his call for the proletariat's might,

---

152. Ambedkarite Buddhism, or the neo-Buddhist modernity of Ambedkar and Gopal Guru, is problematic, especially in light of the groundbreaking release of Evan Thompson's *Why I Am Not a Buddhist*. Slavoj Zizek, a philosopher from Europe, disapproved of Buddhism in its entirety. See Zizek, *Agitating the Frame*.

153. Guru, "One-Dimensional View," 98.

I found resonance in Ambedkar's fight.
Because of the oppression of Caste, there is a divide in classes.
Untouchables' struggle cannot be denied.
John Rawls wore a vast veil of ignorance.
I sought justice without the Caste's cruel stride.
Behind the veil, all are equal, born,
Untouchables' plight is no longer torn.
And Gopal Guru, with deep insights,[154]
Echoing Ambedkar's call to wake from sleep,
For in theorizing Caste's bitter pain,
Untouchables' dignity, they both sustain.
So let us universalize, in thought and deed.
Ambedkar and Guru's works,[155] they plead,
With Western philosophers, hand in hand,
Toward a world where justice stands.

---

154. Guru, "One-Dimensional View," 100

155. Overall, the Buddhist viewpoint of Ambedkar and Gopal Guru is a conservative one that holds that the Untouchables can be freed. Even if they write against caste, their views are rooted in antiquated ideologies. As long as Untouchables adhere to Ambedkar's Buddhism, they can't be liberated. Theology in Christianity is liberating. Analysis is mine.

41. American Philosopher Eleanor Zelliot: Champion of Social Justice

In the realm of sociology, a luminary shines,
Eleanor Zelliot, whose brilliance defines.
An American scholar with an emotional quest,
To unveil the truths society detests.
From Untouchable to Dalit's seminal tome,
Echoes the struggles and invites us to roam.[156]
Through the corridors of Caste, she guides,
Unraveling complexities is where justice hides.
Born of a passion to understand,
The depths of inequality are across the land.
Eleanor embarked on a profound journey.
To amplify voices where silence drowned.[157]
With scholarly rigor and an empathetic gaze,
She traversed the landscape through research's maze.
Documenting narratives, both poignant and raw,
Of a community marginalized by law.
Untouchables, Dalits, Madigas, by any name,
Their plight was illuminated, and their stories became
A testament to resilience in the face of despair,
Their spirit is unbroken, beyond compare.
From her pen flowed insight, like a river's flow,
As she chronicled histories hidden below.[158]
Each page is a testament; each word is a spark.

---

156. Zelliot, *From Untouchable to Dalit*, 84.
157. Zelliot, *From Untouchable to Dalit*.
158. Zelliot, *From Untouchable to Dalit*.

We are igniting change, dispelling the dark.
With unwavering dedication, she stood tall.
I am championing justice and answering the call.
To dismantle oppression, to challenge the norms,
Her legacy endures in academia's storms.
From the ivory towers to grassroots ground,
Eleanor's impact resounds profoundly.
Inspiring scholars and activists alike,
To continue the struggle, to persist, to strike.
Her work contains a clear message.

42. American Philosopher Gail Omvedt: The Light in Darkest Space

In the land of India, where stories intertwine,
A tale of courage, a soul divine,
Gail Omvedt,[159] an American sociologist, bold
With a heart of compassion and a spirit untold.[160]
From across the oceans, she came to embrace
The struggles of Untouchables, their dignity to trace,
In the arms of India, she found her home.
With a black-skinned untouchability, she chose to roam.
Their love knew no bounds, no barriers high.
In a world of prejudice, they stood firm, stood tall,
Gail saw beyond the color of her skin,
In her partner's heart, she found kin.
Together, they lived amidst the Caste's cruel gaze.
Challenging norms in myriad ways,
For Gail, with her wisdom and her vast empathy,
Stood as a beacon against the Caste's Caste.
In the corridors of academia, she raised her voice,

---

159. Gail Omvedt, a renowned philosopher, married an Untouchable with black skin. She is the only Westerner academic who married an Untouchable with a dark complexion, while all other Westerners married scholars or members of the Sacred Caste. She implemented her theories in her day-to-day activities. She followed her anti-caste, anti-untouchability, and anti-racial beliefs into her life, as did John Rawls. Similar to Gail Omvedt, the renowned philosopher John Rawls married an ordinary African woman and died in her honor. Untouchables will always be indebted to Professor Gail Omvedt, just as Africans will always be thankful to Professor John Rawls. Analysis is mine. See Omvedt, *Cultural Revolt in a Colonial Society*.

160. Kumar, "Gail Omvedt."

Speaking truth to power and making a choice,
To uplift the marginalized, the oppressed,
In her studies, their voices were expressed.
Through her words, through her deeds,
She planted seeds of change, of hope's sweet seeds,
Gail Omvedt, with her unwavering grace,
Left an indelible mark in India's embrace.
And though she's gone, her legacy remains.
In the hearts of those who break Caste's chains,
For in her love and her fight, she showed the world
What's truly right. So let us remember
Gail Omvedt's name, a symbol of courage in justice's game,[161]
In her story, we find our call.
To fight for equality, to break down every wall.

---

161. Kumar, "Gail Omvedt."

43. The Sacrifice of Madiga Dandora Voice

In the heart of India's strife-torn soil,
Where Caste divides and tensions boil,
Stands the Madiga Reservation Porata Samithi,[162]
Fighting for rights, their spirits are free.
But in their path, obstacles loom.
As the Supreme Court's judgment casts gloom,
ABCD classification, their rightful claim,
Blocked by power and Caste's cruel game.
Mala and Mahar, untouchable might,
Wielding influence, with all their might,
They hold the keys to the reservation's door.
I am leaving Madigas stranded on unequal shores.
For in the realm of quotas, they reign supreme.
Utilizing privileges, like a distant dream,
While Madigas struggles for a fair share,[163]
Their cries for justice fill the air.
Activists brave, with courage bold,
Their stories are untold, but hearts of gold
They took a stand against injustice's tide.
Even if it meant death, they'd abide.
One by one, they chose to depart.
Leaving behind aching hearts,
Their sacrifice, a solemn plea,
For equality and dignity.
In the face of adversity, they stood tall.

---

162. Muthaiah, "Madiga Movement for Equal Identity," 98.
163. Muthaiah, "Madiga Movement for Equal Identity," 102.

Fighting for rights, one and all,
But the battle rages on with no end in sight.
As Madiga's[164] voices continue to fight.[165]
Though their bodies may lay in rest,
Their spirits live on in every quest.
For justice and fairness, they bravely strive.
In the struggle to keep their dreams alive.
Madiga Reservation, Porata Samithi,
Their legacy burns brightly for all to see.
In the hearts of those who persevere,
Their fight for rights will be forever strong.
So, let us remember their sacrifice.
And honor their courage in all we do.
For in their struggle, we find the key.
To unlock the chains of a caste's tyranny.

---

164. Madiga Reservation Porata Samithi, aka MRPS or Madiga Human Rights Movement Against Exploitation, is advancing the principles that justice Philosopher John Rawls expounded upon in his seminal social justice treatise, *A Theory of Justice*, through their four decades-long democratic campaign against exploitation. Analysis is mine.

165. Muthaiah, "Madiga Movement for Equal Identity," 103.

44. Voice of "Untouchable" Women

The threads of courage are woven into the same fabric as the chains, which are made of Dalit women,[166] and their voices are influential in the presence of silence. In every story, the glow of fireflies carrying the darkness reflects sorrow and courage. Fireflies bear the soul of the whole poem. I will eternally appreciate their suppression story and saga, which I take as a torch. Undoubtedly, whatever we are, we do owe our lightless lanterns to theorists and activists, whose lanterns are the lights that make us see the sorrowful world and the pillars of understanding. They unfurled shriveled fingers as they marched forward towards justice, with each step of theirs bringing relief from slavery. My appreciation choruses up in my heart for the mentors and fellow learners who like whispering cautiously and dancing to the tunes of my passion. Yet you, my reader, avoid that devilish snare of a bystander watching; instead, find your place among the resisters by breaking the submission silence of this piano. United, we hope that "Untouchable woman" will denote pain, despair, honor, and pride someday. Instead, when we hear this, we will think of the sweet melody of victory.

---

166. On March 8, 2024, International Women's Day, I wrote the poem "Voice of 'Untouchable' Women."

45. Voice of Queer

To the courageous souls
whispering resistance, to households
woven with threads of love past
conference, this research echoes your
struggle. It lifts a lantern to the shadows
where discrimination festers, illuminating
the combat for dignity in every facet of
life. From lecture rooms to courtrooms,
from bustling markets to hushed
conversations, it seeks to increase your
voices, woven with personal narratives and
backed via information's unyielding
reality. We stand shoulder-to-shoulder,
researchers and network, for a future
wherein India embraces rainbow shades
with open arms, a destiny in which
equality resonates no longer just in law but
inside the beating hearts of its humans.
This is our ode to a simple India, written
with ink of empathy and fueled by the
unyielding flame of desire.[167]

---

167. In solidarity with sexual minorities.

46. The Indian Ideology

In the heart of India's vibrant tapestry,
It conceals an ideology steeped in mystery.
A complex web of tradition and belief,
But beneath its surface lies untold grief.
Indian ideology is a double-edged sword.
Where ancient customs are deeply stored.[168]
But within its folds, Caste reigns supreme.
A system of hierarchy is a haunting dream.
From birth to death, Caste defines our fate.
Untouchables are crushed by their weight.
Forced into shadows, deemed impure,
Their suffering is hidden and obscure.
Brahmins sit at the top, basking in their privilege.
While Untouchables bear the Caste's cruel task.
Their labor was exploited, and their voices were ignored.
In Indian ideology, their plight is obscured.
From the Vedas to modern law,
Caste's grip tightens, leaving hearts raw.
Untouchables were marginalized, pushed aside,
Their humanity was questioned, and their dignity was denied.
In temples and homes, Caste dictates:
Untouchables were barred behind closed gates.
Their touch, their presence, feared and shunned,
In the name of tradition, their rights are undone.
Indian ideology, a tale of contradictions,

---

168. Anderson, *Indian Ideology*: "Critically from caste and untouchability perspective," 53–54.

Where Caste's oppression meets convictions.
For while we preach unity and peace,
Untouchables' suffering fails to cease.[169]
Critically, we must examine:
The roots of Caste, the pain it's naming.
For Indian ideology to truly thrive,
Untouchables' liberation must come.
Let us challenge the status quo.
And break the chains of Caste's cruel flow.
For until every soul is truly free,
Indian ideology tainted it will be.
So, let us strive for a world anew.
Caste's shackles are finally through.
And in the light of justice, we shall see
A truly inclusive Indian ideology.[170]

---

169. Anderson, *Indian Ideology*.

170. The Indian eminence finds Perry Anderson's *The Indian Ideology*, a thought-provoking work that exposes the real nature of Indian ideology, to be "untouched." However, because he lacks firsthand knowledge of Indian society, Anderson was still unable to adequately convey the Indian mindset. To truly understand Indian thought, one must grasp the essence of lived experience. Untouchables have firsthand knowledge of the crimes against humanity committed by the Indian ideology.

Glossary

Untouchable Caste: Madiga, Arunthathiyar, Burakumin, Panchamars, Dalit, Gahalas, Kinnaras, Rodiyas, Scheduled Caste, Achut, Chandala, Mahar, Chamar

Unseeable Caste: Madiga, Arunthathiyar, Burakumin, Panchamars, Dalit, Gahalas, Kinnaras, Rodiyas, Scheduled Caste, Achut, Chandala, Mahar, Chamar

Unshadowable Caste: Madiga, Arunthathiyar, Burakumin, Panchamars, Dalit, Gahalas, Kinnaras, Rodiyas, Scheduled Caste, Achut, Chandala, Mahar, Chamar

Unapproachable Caste: Madiga, Arunthathiyar, Burakumin, Panchamars, Dalit, Gahalas, Kinnaras, Rodiyas, Scheduled Caste, Achut, Chandala, Mahar, Chamar

Unspeakable Caste: Madiga, Arunthathiyar, Burakumin, Panchamars, Dalit, Gahalas, Kinnaras, Rodiyas, Scheduled Caste, Achut, Chandala, Mahar, Chamar

Walking Carrion Caste: Madiga, Arunthathiyar, Burakumin, Panchamars, Dalit, Gahalas, Kinnaras, Rodiyas, Scheduled Caste, Achut, Chandala, Mahar, Chamar

Walking Carcass Caste: Madiga, Arunthathiyar, Burakumin, Panchamars, Dalit, Gahalas, Kinnaras, Rodiyas, Scheduled Caste, Achut, Chandala, Mahar, Chamar

GLOSSARY

Walking Corpse Caste: Madiga, Arunthathiyar, Burakumin, Panchamars, Dalit, Gahalas, Kinnaras, Rodiyas, Scheduled Caste, Achut, Chandala, Mahar, Chamar

Bibliography

Aloysius, G. *Nationalism without a Nation in India*. New Dehli: Oxford University Press, 1997.
Anderson, Perry. *The Indian Ideology*. Gurgaon, India: Three Essays Collective, 2012.
Ambedkar, Babasaheb. *Babasaheb Ambedkar Writings and Speeches (BAWS)*. 40 vols. Education department, Ambedkar Foundation, Government of Maharashtra.
Balan, B. "Making of Comfortable Exile through Sanskritization: Reflections on Imagination of Identity Notions in India." *Contemporary Voice of Dalit* 11.2 (2019) 84–93.
Barbara, Joshi R. "India's Untouchables." Cultural Survival, Feb. 11, 2010. https://www.culturalsurvival.org/publications/cultural-survival-quarterly/indias-untouchables.
Berg, Dag-Erik. "Karamchedu and the Dalit subject in Andhra Pradesh." *Contributions to Indian Sociology* 48.3 (2014) 383–408.
Brown, P. C. *The Forgotten German Genocide: Revenge Cleansing in Eastern Europe, 1945–50*. Havertown, PA: Pen and Sword History, 2021.
Chakraborty, P. "Gendered Violence, Frontline Workers, and Intersections of Space, Care, and Agency in Dharavi, India." *Gender, Place, and Culture*, 28.5 (2021) 649–79.
Daaham. "The Karamchand Massacre—and the Aftermath." Medium, July 16, 2020. https://daaham.medium.com/the-karamchedu-massacre-and-the-aftermath-dd9f326ff013.
Das, R. J. "Social Oppression, Class Relation, and Capitalist Accumulation." In *Marx Matters*, edited by David Fasenfest, 85–110. Leiden: Brill, 2022.
Davies, Byron. "The Affective and the Political: Rousseau and Contemporary Kantianism." *Tópicos* 59 (2020) 301–39. https://www.redalyc.org/journal/3230/323064336010/html/.
Dewey, John. *Democracy and Education: An Introduction to the Philosophy of Education*. Vol. 4. New York, Macmillan 1916.

BIBLIOGRAPHY

Dirks, Nicholas B. *Castes of Mind: Colonialism and the Making of Modern India.* Delhi: Permanent Black, 2006.

Diwakar, Jyoti. "Sex as a Weapon to Settle Scores against Dalits: A Quotidian Phenomenon." *CASTE: A Global Journal on Social Exclusion* 1.2 (2020) 121–34. https://www.jstor.org/stable/48643569.

Dube, Saurabh. *Untouchable Pasts: Religion, Identity, and Power among a Central Indian Community, 1780–1950.* Albany: SUNY, 1998.

Gilmartin, Sophie. "The Sati, the Bride, and the Widow: Sacrificial Woman in the Nineteenth Century." *Victorian Literature and Culture* 25.1 (1997) 141–58.

Gough, Kathleen. "Indian Peasant Uprisings." *Economic and Political Weekly* 9.32/34 (August 1974) 1391–1412.

Grusky, D. B. "The Past, Present, and Future of Social Inequality." In *Social Stratification, Class, Race, and Gender in Sociological Perspective, Second Edition,* 3–51. New York: Routledge, 2019.

Guru, Gopal. "How Egalitarian Are the Social Sciences in India?" *Economic and Political Weekly* 37.50 (Dec. 14–20, 2002) 5003–9.

———, ed. *Humiliation: Claims and Context.* New Delhi: Oxford University Press, 2009.

———. "One-Dimensional View of Dalit Movement." *Economic and Political Weekly* 30.2 (1995) 98–102.

Hanchinamani, Bina B. "Human Rights Abuses of Dalits in India." *Human Rights Brief* 8.2 (2001) 6–14.

Jangam, Chinniah. *Dalits and the Making of Modern India.* India: Oxford University Press, 2019.

Keer, Dhananjay. *Dr. Ambedkar: Life and Mission.* Reprint. Bombay: Popular Prakashan, 1981.

Khan, D. E. "'It Is Not Possible For Us That Injustice Be Justice.' Some Remarks on the Soghomon Tehlirian Trial at Age 100." *Die Friedens-Warte* 93.3/4 (2020) 268–98.

Kumar, Shailendra. "Impact of Dr. Ambedkar's Philosophy on International Activism of the Dalit Diaspora." *Sociological Bulletin* 71.1 (Sep. 17, 2021) 114-32. https://journals.sagepub.com/doi/10.1177/00380229211030718.

Kumar, Saurav. "Privacy with Respect to Aadhar in Recent Developments." *Indian Journal of Law and Legal Research* 3.2 (Jan. 4, 2022) 1.

Landry, Alexander P., et al. "Dehumanization and Mass Violence: A Study of Mental State Language in Nazi Propaganda 1927–1945." *PLoS ONE* 11 (2022) 1. https://journals.plos.org/plosone/article?id=10.1371/journal.pone.0274957.

Lee, A. "Historical Inequality at the Grassroots: Local Public Goods in an Indian District, 1905–2011." *Comparative Political Studies* 56.12 (2023) 182–85.

Manulak, M. W. "The Sources of Influence in Multilateral Diplomacy: Replaceability and Intergovernmental Networks in International Organizations." *The Review of International Organizations* (2024) 1–32.

BIBLIOGRAPHY

Landry, A. P., et al. "Dehumanization and Mass Violence: A Study of Mental State Language in Nazi Propaganda (1927-1945)." *PLoS One* 17 (2022) e0274957.

Mhaskar, S. "Violence against Dalits in Maharashtra Is not New, but Dalit Reaction to It Is Changing." The Wire, 2018. https://journals.plos.org/plosone/article?id=10.1371/journal.pone.0274957.

Mines, Diane P. "Hindu Nationalism, Untouchable Reform, and the Ritual Production of a South Indian Village." *American Ethnologist* 29.1 (2002) 58–85.

Mukherjee, A., and R. Chakraborty. "Disturbing Trend of Police Brutality in India: A Play between Power and Class?" *International Journal of Law Management & Humanities* 3.4 (2020) 125.

Muthaiah, P. "Dandora 1: The Madiga Movement for Equal Identity and Social Justice in Andhra Pradesh." In *The Journey of Caste in India*, edited by Paul D'Souza and N. Sukumar, 95–115. New Delhi: Routledge India, 2023.

Olcott, Mason. "The Caste System of India." *American Sociological Review* 9.6 (December 1944) 648–49. https://www.jstor.org/stable/2085128?origin=crossref.

Omvedt, Gail. *Cultural Revolt in a Colonial Society: The Non-Brahmin Movement in Western India, 1873–1930*. Scientific Socialist Education Trust, 1976.

Palmer, N. "Genocide." In *The Routledge Handbook of Law and Society*, edited by Mariana Valverde et al., 142–45. London: Routledge, 2023.

Pandey, A. K., and V. N. Mishra. "Dalit Women's Narratives on Sexual Violence: Reflections on Indian Society and State." *Social Change* 51.3 (2021) 311–26.

Pennington, B. K., et al. "A Roundtable on Rupa Viswanath's The Pariah Problem: Caste, Religion, and the Social in Modern India and the Study of Caste." *Modern Asian Studies* 56.1 (2022) 1–64.

Rahman, I. "The Question of Identity: an Analysis of Meena Kandasamy's the Gypsy Goddess, and Urmila Pawar's Motherwit." *The Creative Launcher* 8.3 (2023) 24–42.

Rao, Y. C. (2022). "The Idea of Subalternity and Dalit Exclusion in India." In *Mapping Identity-Induced Marginalisation in India: Inclusion and Access in the Land of Unequal Opportunities*, edited by Raosaheb K. Kale and Sanghmitra S. Acharya, 87–103. Singapore: Springer Nature Singapore, 2022.

Rawls, John. *A Theory of Justice*. Rev. ed. Cambridge, MA: Harvard University Press, 1999.

Schmid, A. P. "Repression, State Terrorism, and Genocide: Conceptual Clarifications." In *State Organized Terror*, edited by P. Timothy Bushnell et al., 23–37. London: Routledge, 2019.

Source Material on Dr. Babasaheb Ambedkar and the Movement of Untouchables. 17 volumes. Dr. Babasaheb Ambedkar Source Material Publication Committee, 1982.

Stroud, S. R. "Excessively Harsh Critique and Democratic Rhetoric: The Enigma of Bhimrao Ambedkar's Riddles in Hinduism." *Journal for the History of Rhetoric* 25.1 (2022) 2–30.

Teays, Wanda. "The Burning Bride: The Dowry Problem in India." *Journal of Feminist Studies in Religion* (1991) 29–52.

Teltumbde, Anand. *The Persistence of Caste: The Khairlanji Murders and India's Hidden Apartheid*. India: Zed, 2011.

Thakur, A. K. "New Media and the Dalit Counter-Public Sphere." *Television & New Media* 21.4 (2020) 360–75.

Thompson, Evan. *Why I Am Not a Buddhist*. New Haven: Yale University Press, 2020.

Thorat, S. "Oppression and Denial: Dalit Discrimination in the 1990s." *Economic and Political Weekly*, 37.6 (2002) 572–78. https://www.jstor.org/stable/4411720.

United Nations. "The Dalit: Born into a Life of Discrimination and Stigma." OHCHR, Apr. 19, 2021. https://www.ohchr.org/en/stories/2021/04/dalit-born-life-discrimination-and-stigma.

Vinoth Kumar, N. "Gail Omvedt: Revolutionary Activist Who Fought Passionately for Dalit Rights." The Federal, Aug. 25, 2011. https://thefederal.com/obituary/gail-omvedt-revolutionary-activist-who-wrote-passionately-about-dalit-issues/.

Wakeham, P. "The Slow Violence of Settler Colonialism: Genocide, Attrition, and the Long Emergency of Invasion." *Journal of Genocide Research* 24.3 (2022) 337–56.

Wankhede, A., and A. Kahle. "The Human Dignity Argument against Manual Scavenging in India." *CASTE: A Global Journal on Social Exclusion* 4.1 (2023) 109–29. https://www.jstor.org/stable/48728108.

Wilson, Richard Ashby. *Writing History in International Criminal Trials*. New York: Cambridge University Press, 2011.

Zelliot, Eleanor. *From Untouchable to Dalit: Essays on the Ambedkar Movement*. New Delhi: Manohar, 1996.

Zizek, Slavoj. *Agitating the Frame: Five Essays on Economy, Ideology, Sexuality, and Cinema*. New Delhi: Navayana, 2014.

www.ingramcontent.com/pod-product-compliance
Lightning Source LLC
LaVergne TN
LVHW051130080426
835510LV00018B/2327